MEMOIR

BORN
OUT OF PAIN

DR. DAVID GLOVER

Published by David Glover

Editing and graphic design by Karen Bowdling

Cover image by stylephotographs

ISBN 979-8-9861431-0-1

Library of Congress 2022908008

Printed in the United States

DEDICATION

This book is dedicated to every little boy whose femininity riddled his society. To the labeled sissy and faggot who sought salvation in the safest organization only to find that there too, he was an outcast.

Also, this book is dedicated to the memory of Ms. Tina Simmons, the precious prophetess who prophesied that I would write this book. I strongly rebuked you, but alas, you were right. May your memory live forever.

ACKNOWLEDGEMENTS

This book wouldn't have been possible without the God Jehovah who first gave me the strength to endure until this point. He truly is my best friend!

-

To my mom and biological dad. I honor both of you as you gave me life and did what you thought was best for me. It's working out!

-

To my first stepdad who transitioned. I visited your grave just last year and said my goodbyes. Thank you for the love you began in me.

-

I acknowledge my biological brother and sister that I grew up with, much love. To my my sister Gwen, although we didn't get to spend time in person, our conversations via the phone was always a bright part of my day. Keep shining from above.

-

I owe an enormous debt of gratitude to those who gave me detailed and constructive comments on one or more chapters, including Kenyatta Sinclair, Jeri Wroten, Frances Baxter, Artravious Craft, Antyon Wallace, Dr. Daniel Black, Brian Jones, Courtney Sinclair, and Majik De Costa. They freely gave of their time to discuss nuances of the text and pushed me to clarify concepts and explain the deeper transparency.

-

I'm also immensely grateful to the churches that allowed me to use my gifts in whichever capacity it was. To Vision Cathedral, Church of the Living God Temple #132, St. Emmanuel, Balm in Gilead Ministries, and Greater Mt. Sinai Church of God in Christ, each gave me immense training and enriching experiences by which I rest my faith and personage on.

-

What an indescribable pleasure it is to friends who become family. First to St. Emmanuel Crew! WHEW! I can say that was irreplaceable! Thanks for covering me and becoming as an armor.

-

To my Milwaukee adopted families, which are plenteous, thanks for staying with me.

-

To Atlanta, which made me grow up and mature in ways I didn't know were possible, much love.

-

To my best friends David Portis, Artravious Craft, and Antyon Wallace, I never would have made it without you.

-

My Atlanta brothers and sisters, chiefly Jerross, Wanda, Ruetta, Mario, Dorrington, Isaac, Thomas, Kurtis, Dwayne, and the memory of my dear brother Pierre, thanks for being my family away from home.

-

To my adopted sons, Jeffrey, Joshua, Jordan, Jason, Justin, Joty, DonJohn, Jarmarcus, and Joseph, I hope to be the mentor and model who points you in the correct direction. Thanks for teaching and allowing into your hearts.

-

To my editor Karen Bowlding, thanks for taking me by the hand and walking me through this process.

TABLE OF CONTENTS

The Conversation...1

Write It Out 4

Mother Speaks 8

Third Times A Charm? 15

You's A Rich White Woman.. 18

Demons...Ha! It's Child's Play 21

Enters The Big One.. 24

Middle School 26

On A Date With...God.. 28

The Death Of James 32

In Walks The Devil Named Calvin............................. 34

Transitional School Drama 39

Basement Church... 47

Boy Meets Dad 49

Community Christian Academy.................................. 54

Mother's Day Prayer 57

Gifts 61

Rooftop Activity 66

College: Final Prayer 70

Dream Of My Mom's Death 73

Go Back To Church 75

What Did You Do With The Money?.......................... 78

My First Assignment 81

Oh, What A Night! 86

The Morning After 95

Daily Enchantment.. 97

Angels Following Me 101

What's Your Job? 104

Pray For The Church 107

Am I Ready For Ordination? 111

Brutish Pastors 113

Pray For The Pastor 124

The Move 128

It Was Time! 134

New York 138

Dreamland: God Wins Again! 145

First Sunday In Atlanta 150

Raped By God 164

Apology To The Church 169

Born Out Of Pain 175

One

THE CONVERSATION

During my home visit in 2010, I had a conversation with my mother. The trajectory of my entire life was changed. Over the summer in Atlanta, Georgia, I began to write my autobiography after a long bout with God.

"Mom, I'm writing my story about the challenges I endured to get to where I am today."

"That's great. Am I in it?" she sarcastically, but seriously responded.

"Yes, of course. I couldn't have arrived without your assistance. I included what I knew about what happened when you were pregnant with me. I'm looking for more stories or events that may be important, but I forgot or don't know."

"Information like what?"

"Well, anything I could've missed. I wrote about being labeled gay because I was feminine as a child. While growing up, I hung around my female cousins. I picked up their feminine traits. My male cousins were older than me and didn't want to be responsible for me. Some were younger than me, and I didn't want to be bothered with them."

As I spoke, my mother seemed to be having a hard time listening. I couldn't determine if she wasn't following or believing what I said. She looked at me in a weird way.

"Say that again!"

"What part?"

I was confused.

With deep thought and concern, she asked, "Say the whole thing over please. I just want to make sure I heard you correctly."

I hesitantly repeated what I told her. Afterwards, my mother passionately swayed her head in disagreement. I tried to figure out what she disagreed about.

"That's not the truth David!"

The energy of the room changed.

"What's the truth?"

"I did only run with Trina, Jaquaye, Jackie, and Tanisha."

"But that's not how you became feminine!"

She shifted her head as she wept. My mom and I had two talks about my homosexuality. The first time she abruptly asked me if I was gay. My mother wanted to know if any of the gay men and women at our church tried to make any advances toward me. I told her they didn't, and we ended the conversation.

A rumor that I kissed a boy outside the back of our church was spread. My mother asked me if it was true. It wasn't, and I told her so. I was nowhere around when the other boys did it. She found out from someone else that I wasn't involved, and we didn't mention the subject again. It was an unwritten rule between us. When my stepfather brought it up, it was to remind me that those with *that spirit* were doomed to hell.

As my mother shed tears, she said, "When you were born, a tiara should have fell out behind you!"

How could a mother say this to her child? What did she mean and how did we get here? I wasn't ready for the comment. Now, the statement she made would have been an offensive *read*. However, from the vibe she gave, and of course knowing my mother, I could tell it was hard for her.

"Everything you did was like a fully grown woman. For example, when you learned to sit up, you crossed your hands one over the other on your knee just like a woman. When you learned to walk, while in your diapers, I could see a grown woman's switch."

I was scared because I didn't act overly feminine. She looked directly at me.

"I was trying to understand how it happened. What did I do to cause this curse on my baby? When I had dates after I broke up with Big David, you came out of the room, and the men pointed and shouted 'Eww, your son is gay! Look at how he walks!' "I was devastated because I didn't know what to do and ashamed because I didn't know how to deal with it."

My mother sobbed. I couldn't walk over to comfort her because I was stunned by the new information. I felt stuck! I had been stigmatized for over 30 years. We ended the conversation. Neither of us could bear to go on. I left. I needed to find a drink! My mind was dizzy with thoughts racing through my head. I didn't know where to begin processing the latest information. I had to rewrite everything, a new narration.

Two

WRITE IT OUT

I woke up and sat in my bed. I was profusely sweating from my head and down my back. I felt like my heart was going to jump out of my chest. I was trembling and heavily breathing. I had a sense of impending doom. What? Not again. I must get this under control. Not again. I was plagued by another memory. In my sleep, my suppressed memories surfaced. I was constantly tormented. Someone opened Pandora's Box and forgot to notify me! Who kept pressing rewind and play on my traumas from my past life in Milwaukee?

I relocated to Atlanta from Milwaukee. I was in a new place and didn't have any responsibilities beyond my education. No one knew me. Well, only two friends also from Milwaukee, but they didn't count. I hardly saw them. I was living in a new city with a blank slate. I didn't have choir rehearsals, meetings, district or jurisdictional, and revivals, to attend. I no longer was committed to the monthly Elder's Counsel. No one was concerned with my church attendance on Sundays. No one could spontaneously ask me to teach a class, emcee a program, direct, or lead a song. No one could question my whereabouts.

I wouldn't run into anyone from the church at the store. Those things are now a memory of what they once were.

With my new freedom, I learned to walk picturesque Atlanta. In Milwaukee I was too busy. I listened to gospel music and walked daily, sometimes more than once. It was my time to think, and I had conversations with myself. This became my regimen, and it was therapeutic. As I continued to walk, I started remembering moments from my past I suppressed. With each step, my mind replayed traumatic occurrences; traumas I chose to bury. I'm not sure what triggered my memories. The memories I couldn't deal with began to seep from the dark hidden places into the light of my consciousness; the recesses of my mind seemed to be on autopilot. My tormenting thoughts moved into my dreams. I unleashed the stream of thoughts, and I couldn't stop them. As I walked, I became overwhelmed with sadness. I could consciously control the pattern of thoughts during the day, but at night, my subconscious didn't cooperate. I couldn't train it to recognize when to shutdown memories when they became too strong.

Here we go again. My sweat poured off my brow. What am I going to do? I cannot continue like this, there must be an out, an answer to this madness. Then, a small voice spoke amid my angst.

"Write it out."

Instantly, I relaxed. I took several deep breaths. I had an opening of light. I could manage what was overwhelming. I stumbled to my computer and logged on. I began to write the memory. I knew about the method of journaling as a therapeutic way to channel emotions. I felt better. Afterwards, each night when I awakened, I wrote. Sometimes, I could only write a line before my emotions got the best of me. As my tears flowed, my vision became blurred. I was blinded and couldn't see the letters on the keyboard as I tried to type. I sat and wept. I allowed my tears to purge my soul. I released my pinned-up agony and pain. I sat in my stuff.

Soon I formed the pages of my memory blogs. It was my testimony, my biography of the ails and trials I endured. Years later, after much contemplation, I decided to move forward with putting my memoir into a format for publishing. My purpose for this literature is not to oust anyone. Neither is it done with thoughts of gaining sympathy. I understand we have had misfortunes in our life. I get it. We can testify and narrate the tragedies. For better or worse, it is with this notion I chose to publish my journey.

As a child, I had personal meditation time. I didn't have any friends, and my older brother and I weren't close. I learned to be alone. My escape was my relationship with God. I spent countless hours in prayer and meditation. During one of those times, I heard the words: Acacia, the worth of your testimony. I didn't know what it meant. I had no memory or reference of the word Acacia. I didn't know what Acacia had to do with the worth of your testimony. I made it my business to look it up. My mother had plenty of resources for me to do research. She had lexicons and concordances. I looked up testimony in the Bible and that is where I began to research the Acacia wood and the Ark of Testimony. As time passed, I better understood its meaning; the personalness of the message from long ago.

This book is a collection of the events, a compilation, where I portray who I am. It is my intent and prayer to inspire and relate to the lives of others. I wish to only uplift, enlighten, and cause awareness. To make it clear how I arrived to this point in my life, I had to go to the beginning, how it all started. Who better to tell it than my mother?

Three

MOTHER SPEAKS

I met a guy when I was 18, and a year later, we moved in together. It was then I learned he was both verbally and physically abusive. Many times, he beat me. One night, he came in and demolished everything in the house. Then, he turned and choked me. Just as I was about to pass out, I grabbed the antenna from the television and sliced his face with it. He let me go. The next morning, my father came to the house. When I answered the door, he walked in and immediately started looking around. He saw how everything was destroyed— furniture, light fixtures, walls, and windows. He turned and looked me in my eyes.

"Sharon! Do you want to stay in this?"

Because my boyfriend was afraid, he hid in the bathroom. I turned and looked at my son who was two. Then I turned back to my dad.

"I wanna go!"

He sent me to Texas. I stayed with my grandparents for a while.

My grandparents kept company in the house. My grandmother cooked for the community. She had big pots of food on the stove, and people came over and helped themselves. Every day, the same gentleman stopped by. He didn't approach. I stayed in a separate room and didn't mingle with the people. About three or four months later, he asked my grandmother if he could date me. My grandmother called me over to her and told me that Lucas wanted to date me. Because of the unlimited trauma I endured, I couldn't answer her. Without saying a word, I left the room. I wasn't ready.

A month later, she approached me and announced that Lucas inquired if he could date me. I told her I still wasn't ready to see anyone. I was trying to get over what I went through with my last boyfriend. My grandmother assured me he wasn't like him. He was nice.

I started watching him from afar. I didn't go near his presence, but I was in eye view where I could observe him. He didn't seem to be a person who was disrespectful or forceful. He was rather mild-mannered, laughable, and personable. After surveilling him for a month, I agreed to go on one date to dinner. I couldn't make any future commitments. I wasn't ready. We had an incredibly good time. We exchanged numbers and constantly talked on the phone. Shortly after, he asked my grandmother if I could live with him. He said he would take care of me. I was firmly against it. I didn't want anyone to think they owned me. I wondered if later down the road, I would meet someone else I wanted to be with. I might feel bad because he could have thought I was using him. I didn't want him to care of me when I wasn't interested in him that way. We talked about the trauma caused by my son's father. He denied paternity and told everyone I was sleeping around. I told Lucas I didn't want more children. He told me he couldn't have children because he was sterile. He was shot while in military service. We ended up having relations one time.

Soon things began to change in the house. My grandmother became more aggressive. I knew then it was time for me to go. I asked Lucas to send me to Milwaukee and he agreed.

It was back in Milwaukee when I started to feel ill, the same symptoms I had when I found out I was pregnant with my first son. I missed my cycle and was sure I was pregnant. Only one person was eligible to be the father. I can't begin to describe the anger I felt. He was eight years older than me and lied. I was manipulated. Like Dante's dad, he knew he was the father but didn't want to have anything to do with our child. I wondered how a person could be so evil!

"If you don't want anything to do with your child, so be it!"

I was utterly depressed and feeling like I couldn't take care of two children alone. I sought a physician to get an abortion. I secured a doctor and privately paid for him to perform the abortion. I was about three months pregnant when I made an appointment at the national non-profit medical center. When I arrived, the doctor was absent. I had to reschedule. While at the next appointment, during my fourth month, suddenly I didn't feel well and had to go to the bathroom. Oh no, I had diarrhea! I cancelled and was ashamed and disappointed. During my fifth month, I went to the local medical center hospital. At the time, the subject of abortion was a hot topic. I had to prepay the doctor. When I arrived, the nurse took me into the room to prepare me and make sure I was certain. I assured the nurse it was best for all parties. I wouldn't have to struggle and watch another child not be able to have necessities and loving parents to raise him. It was also best for his father because I wouldn't have to deal with drama going forward and have to see him again.

After I was prepped for the abortion, the doctor who was to perform the abortion came in and questioned me. He wanted to make sure I was fully stable in making an unalterable decision. I passed, and the doctor went to prepare for the abortion. I fixed my mind not to think of what I was doing, but to focus on the fact that it was necessary. When the doctor returned, they were ready to proceed. The assistant brought in the tools. I lay in position ready for the procedure.

The doctor looked at me and said, "I apologize ma'am. I can't do this!"

"What do you mean? I already paid my money."

"I understand. We will give you a full refund. I'm sorry! I just cannot do it! You should keep this baby. You never know what he will be."

"But you don't understand," I started weeping. "I can't afford to raise him."

"There are other options and help. We can give you some numbers and referrals."

I agreed. With tears in my eyes, I went home and took it as a sign to have the child.

"When I had him, they put him in my arms. I looked down at his little face. That's when it dawned on me what I had almost done. I thought, 'How stupid! What was I thinking! I must have been crazy to try to abort this baby!' When they inquired if I still wanted to go through with giving him up, I was clear on my no! I was keeping my baby. The doctor put the notes in his file, but I had a change of heart."

I used to hold him a lot and weep. Up until my child was three, I watched him and cried. Even when he played with other children, I wondered what would have happened if I had gone through with the abortion. When I saw other children, I wondered if I would have been tormented with thoughts of what ifs? Again, my tears welled. Even though I had the baby, I was horrified at the possibility of not having the baby. I felt tormented.

David was a sickly child. I spent many hours in the hospital because of the chronic ear infections he suffered. He had them every three months. When I took him to the church, I asked for a special prayer because the doctor didn't know what was wrong with him. When he was old enough to be tested, at about eight months, the doctors ran a series of tests. They brought in a specialist to check his ears. They initially thought it was just water in his ears. Finally, they had the results. They called me in and gave me the bad news.

"He has a slit in his ear canal just before his eardrum. This is the cause of the many ear infections. Unfortunately, we cannot fix this, and by the time he is five years old, the gap will grow wider, and he will be completely deaf in his right ear by the age of nine."

Completely heartbroken and a new convert, I told my pastor. He gave me instructions to anoint his ear every day. As well, I was to bring him to the altar every time I came to church. I did and soon noticed a decline in his frequent illness. It wasn't until he was about five when I took him to the doctor for his annual examination. They performed the standard routine check. When the nurse looked in his ears, she quickly left the room. She came back with the doctor who barely spoke and checked his ear. After he examined him, he turned and called other doctors to look in his ear. He began to question me. They had a gadget on his ears while he was playing with the toys they provided.

They explained to me that when children hear certain noises, they will stop what they're doing to try to figure out the noise. He kept playing. They turned it to a higher frequency, and he still didn't respond.

"All babies respond."

Yet he didn't seem to notice the sound.

"Do you have to loudly call him? Do you notice he may answer only when you are on one side of him?"

I didn't notice anything of the sort. They asked if they could schedule a hearing test. I wanted to know the reason for the additional test.

"It appears that his ear canal hadn't properly grown, and it was split in two."

They didn't understand how he was able to hear in that ear. On the day of the test, they put huge headphones on his ears and gave him simple instructions to raise his hands whenever he heard a sound. After the test was complete, the doctors, specialist, and I were astonished by the results. His hearing was far above the normal level. His left ear where the deformity was located, proved to be significantly stronger than his right ear. That was a testimony that spoke of the miraculous power of God.

Four

THIRD TIMES A CHARM?

I entered Milwaukee High School of the Arts, which was engulfed with alternative lifestyles. It was where I learned the basics of the life of homosexuality. I was saturated with the nuances of that lifestyle. At school and church, I was rarely without the homosexual indicators being blatantly placed in my face. With little to no strong male role models in view, it was easy to accept my femininity without thoughts of the need to change or adjust.

Most of the time, I was intimidated by masculine men because I felt they bashed or made fun of me, over and over again. I developed a phobia of being in front of masculine men. I had no clue of it until one day my friend brought me home from college. First, she had to make a stop by her friend's house. She failed to tell me it was a party with straight men. They would have been labeled as thugs or hood. When I walked into the room, I immediately went to an area in the kitchen and stayed. My friend came into the kitchen to get something to eat, saw me, and asked if there was a problem. Of course, I said nothing. She immediately began to dive into my psyche because of my nonverbal response. At that instant, I discovered

I indeed had a subconscious phobia of being around masculine men.

During that time, I was extremely depressed. Nothing made me happy. Going to church was fruitless and school was a chore. Coming home was detestable at best. I felt like my life wasn't worth living. I was tired of being talked about and struggling trying to decide what was right. I heard preachers stand and expound against homosexuality but some of the same pastors tried to *talk* to me or do so for others. I was tired of the hypocrisy in the church and felt I wasn't appreciated for anything but to make people laugh. No one supported me. My family acted like they didn't want me around. I had no friends. Once again, I stood in the mirror crying for what seemed like hours. I had enough. It was a different house and mirror. But I had the same feeling, just a bit stronger. I wanted someone to love me for me; someone to accept me for being me. Was I asking too much? Where was the love God said He gave to mankind? I decided I wouldn't be greatly missed if I left and didn't come back. I was ready to end it.

I walked to the store to get a bag of flaming hot chips, which were my favorite chips. When I returned, I found a bottle of my mother's pills. I decided to take my life. As I stood in my mother's fabric room, I poured the pills in my hand. I heard a voice speak.

"Is this what you want?"

"It will be better than living like this."

As I was putting the pills up to my mouth, I heard a lady praying, "Lord touch that boy who is about to commit suicide. Turn it away."

A strong wind, the hand of God, entered the room and knocked the pills out of my hand. I began to horribly weep. I went upstairs to my room and climbed into bed. "Maybe I will die in my sleep," I thought. I awakened in a pool of tears. I was shaking and felt an overwhelming sense of worthlessness. This was the same feeling I felt that day and for the third time, I tried to commit suicide. I typed...

Five

YOU'S A RICH WHITE WOMAN

A s my only older brother and I were folding clothes in my parents' room, we had small talk. Nothing major, mostly nonsense and child's play. One day, when I was about seven years old and we were doing our weekly chores, my brother stopped folding clothes. He stopped as if something had occurred to him. He looked intently at me.

"What have you done with my little brother?"

I didn't expect he would ask such a thing! We didn't have a previous conversation about it. I was confused and stared at him. I was trying to understand what this meant. I couldn't tell if he was serious.

"Hey, tell me! What have you done with my little brother?"

"What are you talking about?"

"You heard me! What did you do to my little brother?"

"Huh? I don't know what you're talkin bout!"

"Just tell me where you put him or what you did with him. I promise I won't be mad!"

I was without an answer. It didn't make any sense to me. I couldn't get over how earnest and sincere he seemed.

"If I am not your little brother, then who am I?"

"You some rich white woman! I want my little brother! Tell me where you put him!"

He burst into laughter, and I couldn't help but laugh with him. I didn't have a quick retort. But somewhere in my consciousness, I felt enamored with the idea. A rich white woman, yeah! That's right. It was as if he saw what I mostly felt I embodied. For me, it was an answered prayer.

Being rich symbolized that I was to have no worries and expected the finer things in life. I wouldn't be confined to the economic ruins that easily beset my people. I was rich! Being white would've reconciled the position I held in the world. I was above, not beneath. I experienced colorism and discrimination and being white would've meant privileged. I wouldn't have to bow to the constraints prevalent in Black society. At seven years old in Milwaukee, Wisconsin, I wasn't yet familiar with the soft, passive discrimination that lay in wait. Yet, I had a clear understanding. My darkness was a curse, not a blessing.

My brother and I shared a room and had a bunk bed. Because I was the smallest, my brother made me sleep on the top bunk. When we moved, my brother got his own room. My parents bought him a new bed. I inherited the old bed in my room. I continued to sleep on top, perhaps out of habit. We were constantly at odds with each other. I swore he hated me because I acted like a *sissy*. He tried to *man* me up by fighting. Of course, because he was much bigger, it wasn't hard to do. I returned the favor and became hateful and spiteful. He often teased, rather taunted me, calling me fag boy, punk, or sissy. I was hurt and had great disdain toward him in my heart. On top of that, my brother was considered to be a pretty boy. He was light skinned with wavy hair, destined to be a ladies' man. I, on the other hand, was dark, looked like nothing promising.

Today, I still marveled at the thought of people that were rude and trifling enough to say when they saw us together "What happened to you?" as if I had gotten the short end of the stick. I was determined to prove I was just as good, if not better.

Whatever he did, I followed, but worked twice as hard to be much better. My brother asked to direct the choir. I did too. He chickened out. Not me. They stood me on a chair because I was short, and I directed my first song. It was a success! I won. I to this day, still direct and have been blessed to do quite well. He then started playing the congas at church. I asked to be taught how to play the drums and became a part-time church drummer. Through default, my brother is responsible for me acting, leading songs, and most important, learning Scriptures. Funny how my desperation to outdo someone, even as a young child, helped me to mold my life and destiny.

Six

DEMONS...HA!
IT'S CHILD'S PLAY

One night when I was about six years old, I was awakened because of the noises in my room. When I turned to see what was causing the noise, I saw three to four little demons playing in my room. I wasn't quite sure what they were, but I could see them, and they appeared as real as any physical human. They were the size of an average six or seven-year-old. I don't remember their faces. It wasn't important. When they saw me observing them, they stopped their activity and introduced themselves. I told them they were too loud. They apologized, and I went back to sleep. For the following months, they were a regular occurrence. There was no need to tell my parents.

After a couple of months, I encountered my first altercation with one of the demons. As usual, I was awakened to their presence. Once again, I told them they were too loud. One became a tad cocky. They retorted that I should just be lucky to have them in my presence. I knew it was abnormal. I didn't have to take it. I told the demon he didn't have power over me, and that if he continued, I would tell my mother. He called my bluff. I went to my mother and woke her from her sleep. She asked me what was wrong, and I told her what happened.

She and my stepdad were startled. I'm sure they were puzzled. I didn't know how they felt and if they believed me. The pastor told my mother I was a gifted child, and the devil was after me. They called him and handed me the phone. He asked me questions that I don't quite remember. He told me not to be scared and to rebuke the devil and send him back to the pit from whence he came.

I wasn't scared. I was assured that God and my parents would fix it. However, I didn't want to be the one to rebuke him. When I gave them the phone, they asked what he said. I told them they needed to rebuke the devil. My parents informed me that the pastor already told them I should be the one to do it so that when they weren't around, I had the power to rebuke him. I got on my knees and began to pray. As I prayed, I heard the pitter-patter of the demon's feet as he ran from my room down the hall to my parent's room where we were. It stopped behind me and spoke.

"I know you're not about to do this to me...right?"

When I noticed his smugness, my boldness came over me. I got off my knees, faced the demon, and commanded it to return to the pit where it came. Then, the most remarkable thing happened. I saw the floor open, and the demon dropped into an abyss. After that, the demons didn't stop visiting, but I no longer had a problem. As well, the stature of the demons grew to the size of teenagers. The cycle seemed the same. I was often awakened to their noises, and as I turned over, they fell in line, introduced themselves, and told me about their special talents or gifts.

I woke up smiling, remembering one of my earliest memories of my encounter with the demons. I didn't get that they were bad. I walked over to the computer and typed...

Seven

ENTERS THE BIG ONE

One night as I was asleep, I awakened. I was around six years old. Unlike other nights, I wasn't roused because of noises the demons usually made. A radiance of light was in my room. On my stark white walls was an electric blue light with a strong sense of presence. After being awe struck, I turned over and saw a male-figure who was as tall as the room. He had beautiful white hair flowing to the back. He wore the most magnificent cloak of blue, which had a pronounced indentation of symbolic imprint throughout his garment. He held a scepter. Once I had taken in this sight, he spoke. His voice reverberated throughout my room. I thought I encountered the most exquisite wonder of the world. Boy was I wrong.

"Hello, my name is Diana. Will you accept me as your friend?"

For years, that was all I could recall. Later, I remembered that I approved of him. Diana is a girl's name. I didn't understand. I thought it was a boring and ugly name. I said I was going to rename him. He objected and said I was unable to do so. No matter how I tried to cajole him, he flatly contested and refuted my efforts to affix a more suitable name. I asked if

I could add on names while keeping his original name as he wished. He seemed to be okay with it, so I called him Diana Lee Lillian Jackie. Ha! It was the best I could do. Soon after, he left, and the others returned.

They walked alongside me and shared special things and secrets. During that time, I didn't play with toys as the other children. I stayed to myself and of course my unseen friends. I was deeply engaged with music, which was my safe haven. I came to know that Diana coordinated my frequent night visits for training. I was escorted to the lower chambers and training commenced. The *gifts* the little demon friends gave me served as the basis of my training. I learned how to use them in strict exercise. I couldn't thoroughly remember the visit next morning. It was as if there were two sides, one who was the church boy and the other who reported for duty in the dark arts.

From what I recall, several times while in training, a massive hand appeared across the ceiling. Everyone in the room stilled with fear. Then the hand engulfed me. I was yanked into my body. The transition quickly happened. When I was put back into my body, I rose because of the commotion. I heard my mother praying. I got out of bed and followed her voice.

When I found her, she was praying, crying, and pleading, "Lord, save my boys. Don't let my boys die and go to hell. Cover and protect them. Don't let the enemy get a hold of them."

It was years later when I understood it was the power of her prayers that caused the hand of God to come and rescue me.

When I arose, I walked over to my desk and computer. I sat and typed...

Eight

MIDDLE SCHOOL

I was enrolled in a middle school for reading, math, science, and open education for excelled students. The students were tested and divided according to scholastic scores. The four groups were called families. I tested exceptionally well in math and reading. What I didn't know was that the school was a hotbed for witches and Wiccan worshippers. At the time, I was a devout Christian engulfed with the power of God. I encountered witches in a whole new realm. Until that point, the only contact I had with demonic activity was at night and in spirit form. In the family next to mine, there was a community of young witches. As I walked down the hallway and in the locker area of the students, I saw emblems and symbols. My spirit immediately knew they were related to cultic worship.

One day, a substitute teacher for my science class came in wearing an earring indicating that he was a part of Wiccan or cultic worship. As he taught, I kept my eye on him. I was seated alone in the front row. I was easy prey. After he gave us our assignments, he knelt in front of me. I don't know if he got down on his knee so that no one else in the class could hear what he said.

He whispered, "I know who you are."

I was 12 years old. Was he trying to intimidate me? What he didn't know was that I was a sanctified child who couldn't be easily moved when threatened.

I looked directly in his face and countered, "Yes and I know who you are as well, but my God is stronger."

I don't know where I got the ability to say it. I can only rest assured that Spirit of the Lord spoke out of me. He got up and walked away.

I was very feminine. Because of it, I was brutally talked to and treated. I was taunted every day. Lunch trays were thrown at me, I was spat on, and slapped...all because I was a faggot or sissy. I was often jumped as well. For many days, I felt like dying, I wanted to commit suicide. I was coming into manhood, and no one was there to answer my questions or teach me about what was happening on the inside of me. My hormones were labeled as being of the devil. I needed to be rebuked. I had no idea this was normal. I was still saved and refused to fight. In church, I was taught that the Lord would fight our battles. To allow my peers to say what they wanted, be falsely accused, and punished for something I did not ask for felt more than I could handle. It almost took everything out of me. I woke up shaking my head. My life was a mess...I typed...

Nine

ON A DATE WITH...GOD

During a particular time at my church, we went through a curriculum on "Matters of the Heart." The courses were developed by the pastor's wife as inspired by God. The plan was to divide the men and women and have sessions on topics applicable to heartfelt emotions and matters that affected each gender. I wasn't pleased with the idea or the process of the series. I loathed having to speak or deal with any issues close to my heart, in any aspect. I was taught and drilled to be emotionless. For years, I had put my emotions away except for anger, wrath, and rage. I sat through the first night of the session and barely participated and listened. After the session, my aunt asked me how it went. I told her it was not interesting, and I would have preferred to have done something else. The truth was that I was unwilling to surrender that part to anyone including God.

My aunt told me that God was going to deal with me himself. I hated to hear those words. I believe trouble was near. It was like people threw those words around whenever they felt I was being too much for them or myself. I stood my ground. I suffered injury to my heart and endured so much pain. It was more than best to keep my issues locked on an island with sky-high, impenetrable fortified barriers, encased in a moat with live crocodiles, electric eels, snakes, and anything else where I could ensure the fatality of anyone or thing who dared to enter the formidable walls of my heart.

That night, I received a visitation. An angel came into my room while I was asleep and awakened me. I had an appointment with God. I was scared because I thought the angel meant I was dead and was going into judgment. The angel assured and reassured me that it wasn't the case. I kept questioning the angel as we climbed higher and higher in the atmosphere about where we were. I was unsuccessful in every attempt. All I wanted was clarity. What was the reason for an appointment since I hadn't sought God?

Finally, we stopped in what seemed to be nowhere. As far as I could see, there was nothing but white, full plush fluffy clouds. God was seated on a throne next to me. He was quiet. I was seated next to him and faced the same direction. I saw what seemed like a movie screen. It was a movie based in the 1930's. An African American teacher was working with children in the schoolhouse. He poured himself into helping and nurturing his students. One of the young boys got in trouble. When he arrived home, scared of his parents and possible repercussions, he conveyed to his parents that the teacher inappropriately touched him. The boy didn't mean to bring harm to the teacher, he was just trying to save himself. Immediately the father acted. Enraged that his son was mishandled, he went to the community and gathered a heap of followers, seeking justice for his son. They brought guns, bats, and other weapons.

The teacher was alerted that the group was coming and began to run for his life. The men chased after him. He sprinted to the nearby white community where an older white woman was watering her lawn. He rushed to her and asked if he could hide in her backyard. He was desperate and panicked. She agreed. He dashed to the backyard and jumped into the trunk of an old, parked car, hoping they wouldn't find him, or he would die from lack of oxygen. The feeling of despair and agony was as heart-wrenching as the thought of an expected end for something he didn't commit. The angry men confronted the woman, and not knowing what to do with a group of people with guns and weapons of all sorts in hand, she screamed. They tried to ask her where the man went, but she wouldn't hear of it and screamed the more. She was inconsolable. A neighbor called the police. Once the officers showed up, they told everyone to vacate the premises. Irritated and disappointed, they left, unaware of the teacher's whereabouts. Fast-forward 15 years later, it was revealed to the community that the teacher was innocent, wrongfully accused. A board was assembled to decree his innocence, but no one had seen him. Two ladies spoke up and said they knew where he was, and if they were allowed, they would go to tell him the wonderful news about his clearance so that he could come back to the community and perhaps, back to the schoolhouse. They shared the good works he had done and how different the community could've been had he been able to stay. The ladies set out to share the wonderful conclusion to the former teacher. They approached the house where the white lady lived and went to the backyard.

The women found the man seemingly content, humming in the opened trunk.

"Hello," they greeted him.

He looked as if he was surprised but expected to see them. He cordially returned the greeting and proceeded to carry on.

"What are you doing?"

"Umm, nothing. How may I help you?"

He was irritated with the small talk.

"Well, we brought good news to you today. The board of our community discovered they made a terrible and grave mistake over 15 years ago. They sent us to bring you back to the community. Your name is cleared. Would you like your old job back as a teacher? The children desperately need you, and it would be spectacular of you to rejoin us in rearing our children and providing them with a fine education."

In utter disbelief, the man looked at the woman. Without saying a word, he hummed, as if they weren't there.

"Um sir, did you hear what we said? It's good news, isn't it?"

The man stared at them, and his tears welled in his eyes.

"I can't go back there."

"Why not?

"Because I have been here 15 years, and this is all I know. It's good and kind of you to let me know that my name has been cleared, but I don't know the culture of your community. Leaving took more than just my name away, it also took my existence, my life."

I awakened and heard, "Thou art the man," and immediately knew, I was the man! I typed...

Ten

THE DEATH OF JAMES

When I was three years old, my mother married James. He was a preacher and carpenter. He did side jobs and used our basement as his workspace. I learned at an incredibly young age that light-skinned people were privileged, they were preferred. My mother's complexion was fair. Before James joined our family, people looked at me differently. He was dark-hued like me. After they wed, when others met us, they assumed since I looked like James, he was my biological father, and my older brother's father was someone else.

From the moment James walked into our lives, I felt like he appreciated me. I was *his* son. It was obvious and evident. He took me with him and left my brother at home. When we went Christmas shopping, I was allowed to choose several toys, while my brother could select one. In hindsight, the cost of my brother's one toy may have been equivalent to the three I chose. I only remember being the favorite. When James had to clean the church after services on Friday, he bought me ice cream they were selling. I consumed it as he cleaned. He didn't buy any for my brother.

Late one night, I woke up because of the loud sirens and blaring lights. I went downstairs to investigate. Our house was filled with people...medical workers, firefighters, and family. They were bustling between the living room and my parent's room. I saw my mother with my aunt, and she didn't look well. I needed to investigate more. I slipped into my parent's room without being noticed. I saw the paramedics zipping James into a bag. His eyes were still open. It was last image I had of him.

I vaguely remember the funeral. I do recall marching in behind the casket. I thought we were a part of a play. In the play, James was playing dead. He was doing a superb job of not moving. Being young and naive, I had no clue he was dead. When we arrived at the cemetery, my aunt was tasked to watch me. It was a sunny day. I didn't understand what was happening at the gravesite. When they lowered James into the ground, I lost it. It finally clicked. He was dead...not coming back! When I awakened, I wept. I grieved as if it had just happened. While wiping tears from my eyes, I walked to the computer and typed...

Eleven

IN WALKS THE DEVIL
NAMED CALVIN

A year and a half after the death of James, my mother began to date Calvin. At the advisement of the mothers of the church, she introduced Calvin to us. They took us to a popular pizza and children's entertainment business. I was excited to go. Dante and I played and ate pizza to our little heart's desire. After my mother dropped Calvin off, I stood up in the back of the car.

"Mom, you cannot marry that man. If you do, you will just end up in court and hurt!"

I don't know what my mother thought, but I'm sure she wondered why I said it. I had to find my feet and get up from the floor of the car. I was sure to not say it again!

During my mother's second marriage, she tried to do what the mothers of the church told her. "Be a good wife," they said, which meant to be an obedient wife. The church leadership taught that the husband was the head of the house, and therefore had the final say. The job of the wife was to cook, clean, and care for the children and her husband. My mother was to be a doormat.

In our extended family, there were about 10 of us who were cousins. We hung together during family occasions and times in between. Most of the boys were older than me. My brother, who was four years older, didn't want me around because he thought I would be in the way and felt like he was babysitting me. I was the child who clung to my female cousins and played jump rope, which naturally caused me to become a bit feminine.

I loved the church. My mother, being *sanctified*, was always there. One day, while on the altar with a cousin and another child, we received divine prophesies. I was to be a forceful and powerful preacher with a unique anointing. I was about seven years old. I didn't have a clue what being a preacher entailed, much less the details to become one.

While growing up in my house and especially at church, those religious folks made it seem as if the preachers or pastors were little gods. It was inferred that they didn't make mistakes. My mother refused to allow, entertain, or convey in any way, shape, form, or fashion the notion that a preacher could be wrong. I knew pastors who committed sins or had been *sat down* because of open sins. We weren't allowed to utter a word about them or anyone else in the church. It was forbidden to negatively talk about grown folk!

My stepfather Calvin was a devout Christian. He followed the pastor to the letter. Whatever the pastor said was the final word. Every time the church doors were open, he was there unless he had to work. When the pastor preached somewhere, my stepfather was surely there, as well as the rest of us. He often quoted the Scripture, "As for me and my house, we will serve the Lord." We were taught to honor them and respect what pastors said.

I agree, however, I know that it must be taken with the balance of wisdom. I believe that pastors are indeed the mouthpiece of God, but also understand Romans 10:14 (KJV), which it is stated, "How then shall they call on him in whom they have not believed? And how shall they believe in him of whom they have not heard, and how shall they hear without a preacher?"

Soon after receiving the wonderful prophecy, my stepfather decided that if I was going to become a preacher, I would have to get prepared. This, he felt, was his obligation and duty as a parent to train up a child in the way he should go. He decided I should fast every Saturday until noon, which would allow me to yield to God and learn the Scriptures.

Every Saturday, while the rest of my family enjoyed eggs, bacon, grits, pancakes, toast, and sausage, I was left in my room to pray, read the Bible, and give reports on what I learned. I did have a breakfast plate put aside for me when I completed my fast. Who likes three-hour old eggs and grits? His treatment of me was more torture than beneficial. I developed a great distaste to becoming a minister. I didn't ask to be a preacher, nor did I want to be one. My mind was set on being a singer, teacher, or lawyer.

One day, while my stepfather was speaking to the pastor, he told him he had me fasting until noon every Saturday.

"With the type of demons he had to fight, he needed to fast like a grown person."

"Yep!"

You guessed it. My fast was changed from ending at noon to three o'clock. Once that pastor died, his son took over and told my stepfather I needed to have a childhood and learn how to grow like the other young people.

We had Bible study in our house weekly. We took turns reading Scripture verses from one chapter. My father began at the top of the same chapter and commence to read it again, verse by verse with an explanation. Most of the time, I mentally checked out. Whenever I listened, I became frustrated because of the *explanations* he gave. In my humble knowledgeable opinion, I felt his interpretations were stupid and wrong, at best elementary. He lacked spiritual truths. He also led the family prayer every night. I memorized the session. He had a calm beginning. His script was virtually the same unless he breathed differently. After repeating the beginning twice, he transcended into to a harsh glottal voice. I took it to mean he was serious. I often chuckled and wondered if he understood that devils and demons aren't made nervous by loud noises. Neither are they moved because of redundancy or chanting of words.

My stepfather was on every imaginable committee and auxiliary he could at the church. I was automatically included. Because of my wonderful prophecy of becoming a preacher, I had to be properly trained. I was on the witnessing, sick and shut-in visitation, hospitality, and any other team he deemed appropriate for church growth and preparation for pastorship. He also began to drag me around to different revivals and small services so that he could show off my musical and biblical knowledge.

I made my own decisions. I refuted all titles someone else tried to attach to me. I believed I should have control over my destiny, which was both a good and bad thing. It was good because it was one of the reasons I refused to enter the life of homosexuality. It was bad because unfortunately, I was stubborn and felt I had to prove something to everyone and everything, including God. It was a challenge for me to submit to the will of God when I didn't agree.

Twelve

TRANSITIONAL SCHOOL DRAMA

My older brother was having issues at school. He was in middle school and was continuously called to the office for fighting with the other boys in his class. They were jealous of him and picked fights. My parents decided to send him to a different school. While they looked for a school, our pastor and wife suggested Community Christian Academy, which was a local private Christian school they enrolled their grandchild, whom they were raising as their own. With a mere suggestion, it was settled. If the pastor recommended it, it was good as gold. My parents told my brother he was going to the new school.

"Am I going to transfer to the Christian school too?" I excitedly asked.

Being at a Christian school seemed surreal to me. It would've been everything I could imagine. I would've felt right at home, my utopia.

"No, we can't afford to send both of you," my mother responded.

I was devastated and insulted.

"Why does he get to go to the Christian school? He isn't saved like me!" I retorted with tears in my eyes.

How could my parents do that to me? The church was my life. I was a devout Christian, on the battlefield for Jesus. For years, I immersed myself into the Bible. I knew each book and memorized a minimum of three Scriptures per book. I didn't miss a service. The only reason I wasn't at noon-day prayer was because they insisted that I stay in school and eat lunch. I was willing to skip lunch to meet God in prayer. For the life of me, I couldn't understand the cruelty of putting my brother in the Christian school when he was unworthy. What could I do?

"He's only going because he has been getting into trouble at school and has gotten expelled," my mother explained.

The only thing I heard was that my brother was being rewarded for bad behavior. I didn't understand why I was being punished for loving God, for walking upright and toiling in His vineyard. I was livid! I thought if doing bad allowed for my brother to get into a coveted school, then I could do it too. I set out to get into the Christian school by any means. I was steadfast against allowing my brother who was, as far as I was concerned, a class-A heathen to reap the benefits of a Christian education while I remained in the God-forsaken awful school. I immediately started doing bad in school. I was rude and uncaring. I stole free fast-food gift cards from my teacher's desk. Because I was an exemplary student, one of excellence, my deviation caused my teacher to become confused and alarmed. She privately asked me several times if everything was okay, expressing her concern for my poor performance. When she saw she wasn't having an impact on me, she sent me to the school counselor, fearing there may have been something going on at home. It didn't work. My behavior remained dismal. She set up a meeting to discuss the matter of my behavior issues with my mother. The meeting with my mother, teacher, and guidance counselor was anything but smooth. It didn't go well! I lied to my mother about getting the gift cards as a reward for my good behavior, perfect attendance, and high grades. When I let the truth come out about my sudden plunge in behavioral issues and decline in grades, I broke down. As a devout Christian, I felt relieved. I didn't have to lie anymore. I thought I ruined my chance to get into the Christian school based on being a model student or was my behavior bad enough to necessitate a transfer? After the meeting, Ms. Teaporten sent me back to class. She asked my mother if she could privately speak with her about something. My mother agreed. I had no idea what else she could want to talk to her about. I soon found out.

I was unfamiliar with playing with boys. I didn't know the *rules* of their competitive nature or their games. During recess I only played with the girls, just as I had with my cousins. I was familiar with jumping double-dutch and hand games, it was natural for me. When I was in the third grade, I learned a harsh truth. As customary of elementary schools, our class had lunch then recess. The delineation of activities for the girls and boys during recess was clear. The boys were interested in playing tag, basketball, football, and dodgeball. I wasn't interested in any of those games. I wasn't aware of the ways and governance of playing with boys. They liked sports and competitiveness. I had no time for games.

The church leadership taught that no one was ever too young for God to use them. I surrendered my life to the Lord and followed every rule I learned to the letter. I refused to wear shorts because I didn't want my little eight-year-old legs to be a hindrance to anyone. I wasn't going to be a stumbling block to someone's salvation because they were lusting after my legs. I didn't wear gym shorts except when in gym class because it was required.

For many boys, a top priority was to define themselves in stark and direct opposition to any human quality they perceived as feminine. The unflattering scorn they habitually heaped on girls, typically derided as silly, weak, subordinate, emotionally brittle, and physically inept contrasted with sporty, funny, resilient, boys who knew how to have a laugh. Their normative social nature was seemed superior.

Being trusted and accepted by a peer group had an important influence on the possibility of being chosen to participate in certain games and sports, in particular the competitive ones. My male classmates teased me, and the girls liked talking with me. Whenever I was around the girls, they treated me like I was one of them, not like the other boys who they pushed away. The boys made me pay the price. They taunted me by walking past when I was playing with my female friends and sneered. I heard, "All right, girls?" or "Look at that faggot."

Sadly, and predictably, any glimpse of femininity in a boy or man is treated with comparable contempt. It is still widely regarded as a sign of homosexuality. Any boy who fails to meet the standard of masculine normality becomes vulnerable to homophobic abuse or worse; whatever his sexual preference, imagined or real. The direct and conscious bullying of known or suspected gay children in schools is not, therefore, the only good reason for combating homophobia. The same fearful prejudice also threatens the wellbeing of any boy or girl who offends against the conventions of a rigid gender order, which boys themselves police with unrelenting rigor.

In my house, whoopings were a regular consequence as punishment for bad behavior. Spare the rod, spoil the child from the Bible was the motto and mantra in my house.

Calvin always said, "You know you about to get it right?"

I just looked, in a kind of stare, silent while streaming tears of apology. The beating I received for my dishonesty, poor grades, and deviant behavior paled in comparison to the mental anguish that followed. After they felt I had been sufficiently punished with lashes from the infamous belt, they wanted to talk. That is when I learned a greater truth. I knew about my missing assignments and poor grades and how to make the correction. I understood that my behavior and bad attitude in class towards my peers and teacher was piss poor. I knew how to make amends. My dishonesty was only temporal, thus no need to put in the work to correct it. However, I wasn't prepared for what was to come.

When Ms. Teaporten asked to speak to my mother in private and sent me to the classroom, she wanted to alert my mother of her grave concern. She told my mother she noticed when I went to recess, I played alone or only with the girls. She thought it was strange and not good that I shied away from playing with the boys. She thought I seemed frightened about playing with the guys and asked my mother if I had other siblings at home to play with. My mother informed her I had an older brother.

Ms. Teaporten was more perplexed. She thought perhaps if I was an only child or had a sister, it would explain my proclivity for only playing with girls. Ms. Teaporten told my mother she witnessed the other boys teasing me and taunting me. She wanted my mother to talk to me to find out why I chose to only play with girls.

My mother mentioned the conversation to my father. Immediately he was ashamed. He felt as if I was a reflection of him. He sat me down and began to tell me how disappointed he was that I didn't play with the boys during recess.

"Why are you playing with girls during recess?"

"I don't know, not sure what else to say."

Could I tell him I didn't feel comfortable with boys? Did I dare say I could relate to the girls more? What was the correct answer? It was known and understood that my choice wasn't favorably viewed. The tone of voice didn't suggest he was open to a *real* conversation. It was clear to me that the point of the conversation was to express how I was shaming him in front of those white people.

The conversation Ms. Teaporten had with my mother was ineradicable proof, once again, I wasn't good enough. Before I changed my behavior, my teacher already believed I wasn't good enough. She thought I had a problem. It was bad enough the children made fun of me. The boys called me Davisha, Faggy-boy, or whatever myriad of names they could creatively label me. To make a man of me, my brother was also beating me. To add insult to injury, the teacher who I adored thought I was unworthy. Did she let me help her during class because she felt bad for me? I thought she was protecting me from the other boys in class. Did she think the same about me? A plethora of questions flooded my young mind until it numbed.

I heard little else Calvin said. I only nodded to accent submission to get through the moment. He instructed me not to play with the girls. I was restricted to only playing with boys. He also conceived a regimen for every other Saturday. He took my brother and me to play basketball at a local park court. For him, he killed two birds with one stone. He taught me to play basketball and spent quality time with his children. His goal was to get me to be comfortable playing with the other boys in my class. It was nothing more than a check next to the list of behaviors he needed to model for the church, which would've surely made him look picture perfect.

From that moment, I entered what I now know as manic depression. I had no energy to do anything. While I maintained average grades, I was unable to pay attention and focus. Every day I dreaded going to school. I played alone. When the girls, who I used to play with, invited me over to play with them I declined and then found a corner away from others to cry. I plunged into the Bible. God and the church were the outlets that hadn't let me down. I made up songs and played church during recess. I became utterly religious, prayed, and talked to God as if he was my best friend. He was. The church preachers taught that God was a *company keeper* and friend to the friendless. Well, that was me! I used my relationship with God to escape the reality of hell and depression.

Thirteen

BASEMENT CHURCH

Demons and I played church games. It seemed innocent, but they were working during the day to cultivate my gifts. The demons and I went downstairs to the basement to have church. We lived in an area where retired African Americans lived. Children weren't in the neighborhood. I used the mop as my utensil of choice to play the part of an evangelist. After I directed the choir, the evangelist set upright to preach between the washer and dryer. She performed a series of miracles, casting out demons and prophecies. I turned the mop upside down, shaking it around. I used the end of the mop as the hair for the evangelist. I traded roles. I was also the possessed person. I shook the mop as if it was dancing and shouting. I made it fall out and get up do the same thing, over and over. It was a ritual I enjoyed several times a week.

One day, my mother asked me what I did while downstairs. I supposed she was wondering why I was there for so long. Of course, I didn't say much.

"Just playing around with stuff."

She inquired further and met a dead end. I wasn't giving any clear answers. She told me she was downstairs washing and saw the mop stand up and start shaking, moving all over the basement, trembling, falling, and getting back up, several times. I looked at her in sheer amazement. She impeccably described the entire service. But how?

I summoned my demon friends to figure out how she knew. They denied telling her anything. She said she asked the Lord what was happening, and He told her this is what I was doing. I looked at her and stood in awe. I didn't know what to say. I knew my mother to always have some strange ways of knowing things she shouldn't have known. I remembered when we were on punishment, and she called to tell us to turn the television off after we had just turned it on. Another time, she knew we were acting up in school, she appeared and told us she knew we were misbehaving. She asked again what I was doing with the mop. I had no choice but to tell her that I played church with the mop.

I woke up trying to figure out why the memory came up. I didn't particularly experience trauma around that event. I was concerned my mother had access to my private activities. Yet and still, I went to my computer and typed...

Fourteen

BOY MEETS DAD

My 7th grade was an interesting time for our family. My mother gave birth to my little sister. I had been the youngest noted baby boy. To say we all were ecstatic for one reason, or another, was an understatement. Prior to my sister, my mother experienced several miscarriages. With each, a darker cloud came the house. When Miah arrived, the joy of her survival was not to be surpassed. Her father was equally happy. Although he wanted a boy, he seemed just as satisfied with a child. My older brother immediately took to my sister like he was her dad part two. He was sixteen years older, so it made sense. He was her protector, even from me. People asked me over and over how I felt since I was no longer the youngest. I was confused.

The child hadn't taken my place. In my head, I was an only child anyway. Everyone else was a prop. I was God's child. My parents were loaned me. Their job was to supply material things as I prepared for my life of service to the Lord! At the same time, my brother was interested in finding his biological father. I'm not sure what caused it, but to be blunt, he was hell-bent on finding him. He asked my mother questions about locating his father. She wasn't reluctant in giving my brother the information. She was concerned about him getting hurt if his father didn't want him. Calvin was also supportive. He gave full consent to my brother's quest. He said he wouldn't stand in the way of anyone finding their family. He offered to take him to his father if he wanted him to. It was one of the few things I thought admirable about Calvin at that time.

My brother found his father. We lived five minutes from him. The arrangements were made to meet. After they met, Dante was excited when he came home. He was glowing. My mother asked him how it went. Dante could hardly get the words out fast enough. He told her he had two stepbrothers and they hung out and had lots of fun. My mother asked how old they were. It turned out that the eldest was my age and his younger brother was two years my junior. I felt inferior. I thought one of the reasons for not hanging out with my brother was because of our age difference. But clearly, that wasn't the case. Now don't get me wrong. I had no intention or desire to hang out with my brother. I deemed him to be a heathen and hell bound. I wouldn't dare be unequally yoked, even with my brother. However, I did feel some kind of way about him preferring to hang with those miscreants.

Soon after, I inquired about my father. Why should my brother be able to find his father and feel joy and not me? What if I had a family with brothers who I could call my own? What if there was a better family I could associate with. Would they love God? Would I have to convert them? Were they already sanctified? Would they accept me better than my current family? I ruminated over each question. My mother already told me that my father denied paternity when she found out she was pregnant. She also said she knew I might have an older sister. That was all she mostly said about him. The only other comments my mother made to me about my father were positive and affirming. She often said that I was candid and smart, just like my dad, but I got my good looks from her. I didn't realize at the time that her words enriched my view of my father, but she unknowingly revealed her low self-image and self-esteem. When I asked my mother about my father again, she looked into my eyes and took a deep breath.

"Well baby, I am not sure how to handle this. I want you to meet your father, but the last thing I know is he was in Port Arthur, Texas. It won't be the same, and as easy as driving for minutes to drop you off. But let momma see what she can do! Also, I don't want you to build your hopes up if he refuses to see you. I haven't talked or spoken to him since I was pregnant with you. I don't know if he's married and if so, how his new family will welcome a child from the past. He may not have even told his new wife he had another child. I just don't want you to be hurt."

About a week afterwards my mother was smiling when came to me.

"Hey baby."

"Hi mom."

"I have some good news. You are going to see your dad!" He is sending for you. How do you feel?"

"I feel fine."

I was internally smiling. I couldn't hide my excitement. I was going to fly on a plane for the first time. I was going to meet my dad! I wondered what my new family would be like. I began a countdown...

When I arrived, I learned I had a younger brother and an older sister. It was extremely hot, and I wasn't used to it. I mostly stayed inside while my brother played outdoors with his friends. I went to the movies and met my new family. They were nice and commented about how much I looked just like my father. I felt like I belonged. After a week-long stay in Port Arthur, it was time to return home. As I was packing to get ready to fly back, my dad gave me an envelope and told me not to open it, but to give it to my mother. When I got home, I gave the envelope to her as instructed. I told her how everything was good, that we had pizza and went to the movies, and he took me shopping and I met my cousins, aunt, and uncles. I went to bed excited, except I couldn't sleep.

In the middle of the night, I heard my mother on the phone. I crept around the corner and eased up to the door to listen.

"Dad, I don't understand! How do I tell him his own dad doesn't want him? He was happy when he got home. He's gonna be devastated!"

I thought my world was coming to an end. I couldn't believe it. How was it I failed? I tried to understand where I went wrong. Did I walk with a switch? Others always had a problem with it wherever I went. I was given a chance and I blew it! The pain in my heart was almost unbearable. I was such a failure. Once again, my *gayness* ruined yet another opportunity. I don't clearly remember how my mother broke the news to me. It is such a blur. I learned to relocate myself in my mind whenever either of my parents were talking to me and I didn't want to hear what they were saying. That was certainly one of those times. I was rejected by my peers, other adults, my stepfather, and brother. I was being rejected by my biological father, not once, but twice.

When I woke up, I felt pain in my heart, as if I had been cut deep and alcohol was thrown into it. I had an immense pain. I was wheezing while trying to breathe through reliving the pain of abandonment. I made it to my computer, and I typed...

Fifteen

COMMUNITY CHRISTIAN ACADEMY

I was more than ecstatic when I transferred to Community Christian Academy. My plans worked. God turned it around in my favor. I was sure it was because of the praying and fasting I had done. God hadn't forgotten my labor of love. On the first day my brother and I walked to school, I was excited. I ran ahead of my brother because I could hardly wait to get there. They opened the day in a chapel where morning devotion was taking place. As they sang the opening song, recited the opening prayer, and read Scripture, which was akin to the services at my church. I was in utopia, the trouble from the previous years at the public school was over. It had all been worth it.

I noticed a Caucasian woman playing the tambourine. She didn't quite play it the way I was trained. I prided myself on being an excellent tambourine player. I simply walked over to her and asked if I could show her how to play her tambourine. She looked at me oddly but allowed me to play. I played it the way I was accustomed to. In the Pentecostal church, we played with intensity. Every Pentecostal church had a person in the congregation who played the tambourine as if God was taking score. With the frequency of the tambourine cymbals, we knew how *lit* the service was getting. When a tambourine player had a slow, steady rhythm, the pastor was preparing for an altar call. When the tambourine was being beat like it personally denied us reparations, we knew it wasn't long before the Holy Ghost arrived. Traditionally, tambourines were a signature instrument to the black Pentecostal church. For me, it was serious! Within ten seconds, the lady snatched her tambourine out of my hand.

"You're going to break it!" she vehemently said.

"No! That's how you are supposed to play it."

"Well, you are going to have to bring your tambourine and play it!"

"Fine!"

I walked back to my seat. She didn't know I was a proud owner of a tambourine that I could bring with me to school. When I got to my class, there were only five of us. I was used to 30 other classmates. Scriptures were used in every subject. They found a way to tie God into each one. It was amazing. It felt like a daily Sunday school class. Everything was blissful and different...except recess.

For recess, students were divided into blocks of classes and age groups. It was at that point I reentered the same anxiety I previously experienced at the public school. Somehow, the gender issue during recess was inescapable. I couldn't hide behind gospel songs and none of my Scripture retorts could cover the ineptness I felt when the boys went to play kickball or tag football and the girls went to play jump rope. To resolve the issue, I found a huge boulder at the edge of the playground near the street. I brought my tambourine and stood on the rock during recess. I sang church songs and played my tambourine. When the teachers on duty asked me what I was doing, I told them I was standing on Elijah's rock and doing the work of the Lord by ministering in song to those who passed by. I wasn't sure what they thought about it, but they did allow me to continue. The other children made fun of me. I didn't care. I was committed to standing on the rock, day after day, singing Zion songs. It's what I told myself to avoid dealing with the issue that I got into trouble for at the last school. Once again, I chose religion as my escape and coping mechanism.

I awakened with a smirk on my face. I was tickled knowing just how serious I was while playing my tambourine on a massive rock. I couldn't help but remember with fondness the times my differentness was my banner. The marked church boy had a God who accepted and loved him...I think. I walked to my computer and typed...

Sixteen

MOTHER'S DAY PRAYER

Under the leading of our pastor's wife, we began to have morning glory prayer, which was done every Sunday, approximately one hour before Sunday school began. The elders, missionaries, and praise leaders were placed on teams and those to lead the prayer rotated. Like most churches, we usually showed up when it was our turn to lead the prayer. One Mother's Day Sunday, I was in charge. My mother and I loved each other but we weren't close. We spoke on a need-to basis and occasionally, just to check on each other. On average, I probably spoke to her about three times a year, besides holidays and Mother's Day.

I was the only one there as I began to pray. I usually preferred it that way because then I could pray as I wanted without the consciousness of someone else being there. As I was praying and singing hymns before the Lord, I prayed for the service, church at large, and for the mothers of the church since it was Mother's Day. I then thanked Him for my mother. I suddenly felt a pain hit me in my gut. "What is that Lord?" I tried to continue but was unable to. The pain was great!

"You must deal with your anger against your mother and be healed!" the Spirit spoke to me.

I hadn't paid attention to the details of how I felt about my mother. For most of my teenage years, the emotions I expressed about her were rage, anger, and hate. Again, I dearly loved my mother, but she didn't protect us from her husband. He was evil at best and caused so much damage to my world while she just stood around and allowed it. She ran from the church and allowed them to win. My mother's motto was that she would rather hurt than hurt someone else. I often witnessed my mother cry because of what the church people had done to her. She accepted false criticism and undeserved blame, done by those who were in authority. They used the microphone as a weapon to vent and throw off onto others while aggrandizing themselves or those in their cliques. My mother was a singer in the church. She sang and led songs on the local and state level. I saw firsthand the hypocrisy of the church leaders. At that time, the church was small and family oriented. Those who dared cross the family had a real awakening coming to them. If you opposed them, whether right or wrong, you were going to pay. It was clear my mother wouldn't stand up for herself. She chose to internalize her pain and hurt.

I on the other hand took the opposite approach. My motto was different. As someone was opening their mouth to speak something vicious to me, I would've killed them with my words. In some ways, I felt my mother was sort of a coward for allowing others to disempower her by their thoughts, opinions, and words. I often wondered how much better our lives would've been had she stood up for herself and children.

My mother was from the old school and believed women had virtually nothing to say in the house. Whatever the husband said was final...without question. They took Ephesians 5:22-24 out of context. Paul said the man was the head of the house, but they aggrandized it to make women feel like slaves versus a help meet. This was a horrible mistranslation of the Scripture as well and a dishonest dividing of the word.

What God was trying to get me to see was that I needed to recognize my feelings toward my mother. God couldn't heal what I wouldn't reveal. I hadn't come to the place where I was able to deal with my emotions. Being that I was a momma's boy, it was a traumatic experience. My mother was an intricate and pivotal source in my life. Although we didn't often speak, I couldn't imagine my life without her. I was also mad at myself for being upset with my mother. I understood her predicament. I knew all too well the conditions she operated out of; however, I just couldn't help but believe she could've done it differently. I suppressed the matters instead of dealing with them because I felt stressed. The spirit brought me face to face with it. I wasn't ready to deal with it. I got off my knees. While in tears, I nearly stumbled. I wasn't going to be forced to deal with what I hadn't chosen to do so. I shut the bathroom door. Immediately, the spirit of God took hold of me, and I flew against the wall. He began to tell me I must deal with it and let it go. Hurting people only hurt people. I rebutted that I didn't want to. Rehashing memories and the pain was too painful, more than I could bear.

From wall to wall, I went until I finally gave in and told the Lord that I forgave her and would release her in love and forgiveness.

As soon as I said those words and did it, my body felt His hand unclench me. He then told me to fix myself and wash my face because Ora was coming. I got up and did as the spirit commanded. Like clockwork, when I finished, Ora knocked on the door and asked if I was okay.

I woke up and sat on my bed. I felt the same tormenting feeling I did on the day of prayer. I wondered if I had fully forgiven my mother. Did I release everything? I typed...

Seventeen

GIFTS

One night, I had a dream. I was entering a church to attend a workshop. The church was like an old Catholic style building with roughly 1,500 seats. I entered the sanctuary where about ten people gathered. As I walked to the front, I saw someone I knew. She seemed excited to see me and to be there.

"Oh David, I am excited we are going to make a compact disk. We can make duplicates here and get exposure..."

Her words seem to fade as I surveyed the room.

The facilitator was a woman who was dressed in a flowing gown, almost like a cape or robe. It was plain and stark, but I was interested in it. Several chains with medallions were hung from a tree-like object, apparently made for the purpose of holding the medallions shaped in the form of the treble clef, bass clef, and other musical affiliations. Stacks of at least 10,000 loose discs were neatly lined in the front of the room.

While sitting and waiting for the workshop to commence, I kept feeling like I had been there before, as if I witnessed the scene. I pondered and looked around.

"Come everyone, get a medallion, and put it around your neck. We're going to love Him, worship Him, and adore Him, and He will give us His blessing and strength and prosper our ways."

The facilitator addressed us in a chant-like manner as people picked their medallions and put them around their necks as instructed. I felt desperately uncomfortable in the setting and didn't want to participate in the procedure. Who was this woman? Where did she come from? Why was she dressed as such? I first didn't understand why we were having a workshop in the sanctuary. I don't recollect signing up for the class. I couldn't help to shake the feeling of previously being there. I was without a medallion, and there was just one left hanging on the tree. The facilitator looked at me and motioned for me as she continued her chant.

"We're going to love Him, worship Him, and adore Him" and He will give us His blessing and strength, and prosper our ways."

I denied the opportunity and sensed her severe disapproval. From that moment, she kept her eye on me. Once she ended her chant, I wondered who was the Him she spoke of. She told us about the different things we were going to learn regarding music and how they were going to make discs. Something clicked in my spirit. It was a trick. She was indeed a witch who was going to perform a ritual and assign us into the field of Gospel music to sabotage it and cause confusion. The medallions were infused with demons and persuasive streams of powers so that each member would have a connection with the underworld. That access would be granted to the demons of choice per medallion. When one was asked to come and get the medallion and place it around their neck, they were, in essence, not simply accepting a piece of jewelry, but rather the demon, rites, and governing of the curse of the jewelry. Placing it around their neck would be to bind them to the policies of the *gift*. Witches used a ceremony on tangible objects to produce intangible results. This is a common and sometimes ingenious ritual to spread demonic activity beyond the reaches of the witches themselves. Now, of course we know this practice was first, and has its origin with God Jehovah. The demonic influence simply stole it and used the principles for its benefit.

I was there before. I saw the training. The other times, I was on the other side. But this time I was converted. I figured out why I was there, which was to disrupt and abort the ceremony. I felt anxious. I didn't know what was going to happen, but I knew drama was to follow. Just as I was finishing my inner consultation, the facilitator spoke to me.

"Is there something troubling you?"

"As a matter of fact, there is."

Just as I was starting to oust her real intent, a young boy in the front row began to levitate. I stopped talking to witness what was going on. The boy, who seemed to be around twelve years old, was levitating in the middle of the air, positioned in an Indian seated style. The witch gave a nod, and the boy faced me. With a slight motion, he sent the discs spiraling my way in what seemed to be lightning speed. I winced and threw up my hands to cover and shield myself from the imminent impact. To my amazement, the disc boomeranged to the boy. Just before impact, the disk stopped and suspended in the air. Then they perfectly aligned themselves and stacked back into the perfect order they were originally in. I gawked in disbelief.

"Yes, that's right, he has the same nine gifts you have. The difference between you and him is that instead of fighting them he learned to train them for proper usage."

Those words rang in my soul, but I had no time to ponder on them because my friend began to say she no longer wanted to be a part of whatever was going on. She was getting her things and was going to take the medallion to the witch. The witch nodded and the boy sent one of the discs toward my friend's head. It spun like a mill and almost cut into her scalp. I immediately ran to my friend and told her to get out as I stopped the disc from sawing into her head. The witch became irritated and chanted over the medallion that was still on my friend's neck. It was like she activated its power or used mind control. She turned to the boy and said that he would pay for failing in his attempt to kill my friend. The same disk was redirected toward the boy. He screamed out in pain from being tortured. I ran to the boy and tried with all my might to pull it back the other way, but I couldn't stop it. Whatever power she had was greater than the young boy. I began to bind the powers that caused the force of the disk to spin, and it slowed down. I was able to eject it from the boy's head. I decided it was time to go! I headed for the door, turned to my friend, and told her to come on.

"I don't want to go. This may be my only time to get a record deal and I have some songs I need to record"!

I couldn't believe what I was hearing.

"Did you just see what happened here?" I protested. "C'mon it's time to go!"

"No, just go on without me. I will be fine."

She broke my heart. She was under demonic influence and her reaction reflected her heart. She wanted a record deal and the fame more than the God who could give it in His time. She was blinded by her desires and lacked sound judgement.

As I was nearing the door, from my peripheral vision I saw the witch turn her attention to me. She began to chant. I had an overwhelming sense that demons were weighing down on me. My motors and faculties began to slow. I had to fight to keep moving. I was determined to get out of the place. I began to plead the blood of Jesus. It became harder and harder to keep pleading and finally I couldn't say it but kept thinking it. I made it to the door. When I reached the outside, I nearly collapsed with relief. I got up and the spirit in me, fully charged from the battle, turned me, called out of me the curse, and sent it to the ground from where it came. I turned and ran as fast as I could from that place, not having an idea for doing so. Behind me I heard a loud thud and fell to the ground. I rolled over and saw the church I came out of in flames. I awakened with similar feelings of fear but without anger. I wonder why it reappeared in my memory. Was I still stifling my gifts? I went to my computer and typed...

Eighteen

ROOFTOP ACTIVITY

My stepfather was a deacon at the church where I was raised. Part of his responsibility was to clean the church, and he took it seriously. It was a weekly family activity. It wasn't just a wipe down or vacuum. Not at all! It was a full-scale, all-out ceremony unto the Lord and thus most sacred. He was systematic and arduous in the rhythm. The intricate tedious process took no less than four hours. Everyone had a list of duties to complete. At first, four of us shared work. After my brother left home and my mother was unable to help, the load was divided between my stepfather and me. Our cleaning quickly developed into a seven-hour chore. My father's work always extended about two hours more than mine. During that time, I sang songs or read the Bible. Sometimes I created plays or acted out church scenes while I waited on my stepfather to complete his tasks.

One evening, after I completed my chores and was waiting on my stepfather to finish, I began to read my Bible and pray. I didn't realize the relationship I was building with the Father during that time. It was simply something to do while I waited. I just figured since I was in the church, I should do some spiritual maintenance, and church was all I knew anyhow. It became my default pastime. In the church front entrance were two glass doors. One was to the main sanctuary and the other to the restrooms, dining hall, and kitchen. Further back was the access to the pastor's office and a flight of stairs to the entryway of the sanctuary.

As I was reading my Bible and meditating, I kept hearing the opening and closing of the door and footsteps on stairs. I turned around but didn't see anyone. It was quite late. I was a young lad at the time. I knew several of the parishioners of the church had keys and sometimes they came to check on us to see if we could use their assistance. My stepfather enjoyed the time of cleaning it himself, so he turned down their offer. I listened for voices upstairs where my stepfather was, and when I was unable to hear anything, I returned to what I was doing. Maybe I just imagined the whole thing. Shortly after, I heard the door being opened and footsteps on the stair. I turned around but didn't see anyone and listened but didn't hear anything. I turned and began to pray. I started feeling uncomfortable and a little anxious. Again, I heard a sound. I went to investigate. I walked up to the door, but it was locked. I turned toward the steps and eased up the stairs, intently listening. Nothing! I looked through the divider that was used to separate the sanctuary from the entryway. I only saw my stepfather's vigorous cleaning activity.

I was confused. Had I imagined the sounds over and over? I turned to the only one I knew who could clear it up for me.

"God, what is going on?"

"Go outside!"

I was hesitant to follow that instruction. I knew it would be a disapproved action by my parents. The church was located across the street from the projects, and it was quite late at night. My curiosity was stronger than my sense of character and obedience to my parents. As I approached the glass doors, without thinking, I opened them and went outside. I walked a couple of steps from the door and looked around. I didn't see anything noteworthy.

"Turn around and look up."

I followed directions. When I looked up, I was awestruck. On top of the roof of the church was a sight I hadn't seen or could've imagined. Huge angels were on top of the church. As I peered closer, I noticed some activity. It was a fight or wrestle of some sort. It wasn't just angels up there. I spotted huge demons. The angels were fighting them. The angels weren't coming from heaven, they seem to be coming up out of the top of the church. It wasn't logical. Angels who were servants of God should be up in the heavens with God. Why were they coming out of the church? God, being sovereign, knew my thoughts and questions.

"These angels are the result of the prayers of the members of the church. They are praying under the guidance of My Spirit. The requests they are making are the instructions being followed by the angels."

I thought it was a fabulous and novel concept. Was what the saints praying for caused angels not to descend from Heaven, but rather ascend out of the church?

"The prayers that are being prayed are for the church to be endowed with the anointing, that the seats would be anointed, and for the choir stand to be anointed. They've asked that when the people come in the door for the anointing to meet them at the door and let them feel My presence as they pass through the threshold of the church. That is why you see the angels coming up from the church onto the roof where they are battling the enemy who wishes to plant his seed and place his evil plan in operation."

I stood in awe while looking at the sight unfolding before me. I am unsure about how long I stood and looked but I'm sure I was there, transcended and marveling in it as God allowed my eyes to see and my heart to perceive. When I awakened, I was smiling. There was no pain, no anxiousness. I felt assured. I wasn't certain why I had this memory, but I was happy it was one of peace and not trauma. I walked over to the computer and typed...with a smile from the inside.

Nineteen

COLLEGE: FINAL PRAYER

Looking over my life and feeling an abyss of insignificance, I had done all I could to make my life feel like it was worth living. I had done all they told me to do in church—never lying, never stealing, never fighting, or even sticking up for myself. Those were what they told me to do, and if so, God would fight for me and abundantly bless me. Well, where was my blessing, my breath of fresh air? I had been duped and tricked. If God was so strong, then why was my life a living hell? From my family at home, church, and school, everything that was connected to me only rejected me. I couldn't get a break. Seek ye first the kingdom of God and all of his righteousness, and all these other things shall be added unto you had failed (Matthew 6:33).

I was a devout Christian from my youth. I happily went to every service. Unlike my brother, I had served faithfully in the choir, junior usher board, youth board, drummer, and every other thing they allowed me to do. I read my Bible every day and read the entire Bible at least three or four times. I did everything by the book. I was the epitome of sanctification. I had given up the folly of my youth and dedicated it to the Lord.

The Lord was to be my stay, my strength, my buckler, my shield, yet I couldn't have felt more abandoned, more uncovered, and exposed. I felt an overwhelming surge of hopelessness and disparity. I blamed God for it. My whole life was one of a fight lost before the fight started. What more was I to do? What more could I give? No longer did I want to be the devout Christian. I didn't care to have a connection with He who formed me. How dare God allow me to suffer without aid and then ask for me to do something for Him. Where was He when I needed him? How dare He give me a free will to do what I want but then tell me that I must do what He wanted? How critically ill and misinformed was He?

The more I thought of it, the angrier I became. I was livid and wanted him to know the damage He had done to my world. The worst part was that I couldn't do anything about it. The events were over, but the pain reigned in my mind. I no longer lived with my family that brought me much agony, but the sirens of the effects resounded like trumpets in my heart. The rejections were like a dagger in my spirit. I made a decision. I wanted to tell God just how I felt. He needed to know the discomfort He caused and agitation He allowed to ensue in my life. The endless disappointments, the gray dismal traces of heartbreak that laced the heartbeats of my life had to be communicated to the God of the Heavens.

To ensure I would be heard, I got on my knees and began to weep. I didn't want to, but I was driven to that point. I had to. I told God in no uncertain terms how I hated Him, and it was a mistake to ever trust Him, for He, like everyone and everything else in my life, had failed! I gave my heart to Him and saved myself while everyone else did what they wanted to do. I expressively told God that He is maybe mighty, and I believed He was, but I thought I would try it another way. I asked if He would refrain from coming near me or touching me. I didn't desire Him to come to speak to me and commune as He had frequently done. I didn't want to smell His aroma as He entered the room. I additionally requested that He take the gifts he gave me. If He decided to take my breath, it was a price I was willing to pay. I was not suicidal but wanted Him to know the utter disgust I felt about His name. I knew I was taking a significant risk. I desperately wanted to get out of my condition.

I felt an incredible surge hit my body. I wasn't sure what it was, but I didn't feel any better. I felt worse. I crawled into bed and went to sleep. The next morning, I awoke and felt the same, but things were a tad different. When I sat up from the dream, I sat still. The whole house was dark. It was tranquil. I could hear the hollowness of my soul. Its emptiness echoed a woeful sorrow. I had no words to utter. It was the darkest moment of my life. I typed...

Twenty

DREAM OF MY MOM'S DEATH

S oon after I asked God not to come near me and embraced the dark force, I had a dream. My mother and I were at a church banquet in my dream. We were the only ones upstairs. My mother was finishing getting dressed and asked me to zip the back of her beautiful evening gown. I went behind her and while zipping it, a man wearing a mask entered the doorway, pulled out a gun, shot my mother, and left. I was stunned in awe and breathless as I saw my mother collapse to the ground. I couldn't decide whether to run after him, tend to my mother, or call downstairs for help. I turned to the phone to call for someone to call 911. I picked up the phone, and there was no dial tone. I immediately hung up and sobbed. I awoke from the dream.

I became angered. It wasn't that my mother was shot. It was because I asked God not to come near me. I made a personal plea with him to take the gifts He had ever given. I had enough inhabited demons to keep the other ones under control, but I still had access to the gifts of communicating by dreams. I called my mother and asked if she was alright. She told me she was, but I sensed something was wrong. I asked again, and she confirmed she was fine. I told her I loved her, and she said the same to me. The same night I dreamed that, her husband of fifteen years told her he didn't love her anymore. Ah, he was the man who shot my mother in my dream. She asked him when he fell out of love with her. He said after the second year of marriage. Blow number two. She inquired why he stayed with her for all those years if he didn't love her. He responded he did it because the church people idolized their marriage, and he didn't want to disappoint them. I awakened feeling hurt and guilty. I was so engrossed in my own pain that I couldn't be as concerned with what the dream meant. I was only outdone with God *forcing* himself over my direct request.

I considered it funny that as churchgoers we can create such an environment with our thought patterns and commentaries. It is true. We must be ever so careful what we do and say because we don't know what a person or family is going through at home behind closed doors. I walked over to the computer and typed...

Twenty-one

GO BACK TO CHURCH

From the point after the dream of my mother's death, everything was a blur. I went through some humdrum calisthenics of everyday life. I occasionally went to church and because of my love for gospel music, I directed the University Gospel Choir and was a licensed gospel deejay. I can honestly say my life began to become more routine except I didn't want a savior in the process. My life began to become increasingly worthless. At night, I began having chronic headaches. Then I started having them every day. I used the medicine I had as well as my friends. I decided to go to the campus medical clinic to see if they could prescribe me something stronger than what I could get over the counter. I went into the exam room and the doctor came in to ask what my problem was. I told him I had a history of migraine headaches and they returned. He asked about my schoolwork load and other stress-related factors. I assured him it wasn't stress and simply told him I believed I had short stints or bouts when my head just hurt, and I took medicine and muddled through it till it was over.

He told me to take a piece of paper upstairs and they would take care of me. I was relieved it didn't take long and rather excited because I was going to get some pills to help ease the pain. When I reached the door to open it, I noticed a placard. It was the psychologist's office. I was quite puzzled as to why I needed to receive my prescription from that office. I went to the receptionist area and told her I was there to get my prescription filled. I handed her the piece of paper the doctor gave me. She took it and looked at me a little strange. I asked her if there was something wrong, and she responded that it wasn't. She told me to have a seat and the doctor would be right with me.

When I walked into the doctor's office it appeared gloomy. I felt alright, despite my nagging headache. As I walked into the office, I saw what looked as if it were two big black eagles on the curtain rods. When I sat down, an invisible force seemed to push me further into the seat. I felt a tremendous weight on my shoulder, and I immediately felt an overwhelming sense of sadness.

The doctor began to ask questions about my living situation, family, and friends. After what seemed to be forever, he asked me about the church. I thought it was different but if he wanted to discuss it, I was willing to divulge the information as well. Then he asked strange questions pertaining to my emotional stability and thinking patterns of my day. He seemed to be probing to discover what was triggering my headaches. I had taken a couple of psychology courses and I recognized some of the concepts and patterns of questions. He then told me that my headaches were due to the high amount of stress I was under. He wanted me to come back every other day to meet with him. I thought it was an awful lot of visits. Once a week or in severe cases twice a week was the average. But he was asking for it every other day. I did mention to him it was a bit excessive. He told me he feared for me. I asked him to explain. He told me I was in a state of manic depression, which was the highest form. According to him, I was masking it and suppressed many issues. He was unable to determine my triggers, which could cause me to snap and commit suicide. I stopped him. I heard him first use triggers in the plural and asked if that was how he determined I was suicidal. He confirmed both; several sparks could cause me to indeed take my life.

He asked me to sign a form, kind of contract, agreeing not kill myself and to call a specific number the moment I wanted to do it. I thought it was odd when he told me to consider going to church for therapy. I asked him what he meant. He believed that church was a place of solace where I found strength, pleasure, and relief.

"And what about my headaches?"

He gave me two prescriptions. One was for headaches and the other was for mood depressants. I called my mom. She told not to take anything. She instructed me to flush them down the toilet. I surprisingly did so.

Twenty-two

WHAT DID YOU DO WITH THE MONEY?

I was sixteen when I went to college. I didn't recall my stepdad saying goodbye.

Since I could remember, he often said, "Get a college education so I wouldn't have to work the white man's job."

My mom, aunt, and cousin drove me to the dorm. It was about a two-hour drive. When we arrived, they helped me unpack my stuff and basically wished me the best. My stepdad had already warned me: "You gone have to find your own way back and forth from college, cause I'm not putting all those miles on the car." They just purchased a brand-new car. He meant what he said. They didn't come to get me or drop me off at school. I had to coordinate rides with friends when I wanted to go home or return to school. Once, I couldn't find a ride back to school because it was the beginning of the spring semester. Everyone had their things and didn't have room for me. By the time I was able to return, I ended up having to withdraw from the whole semester.

One evening when I returned to my dorm, I saw the message indicator light on the answering machine. Because I hadn't paid the bill, I could receive incoming calls but not make outgoing calls. The message was from my stepfather. He said that it was important and to call as soon as I got the message. I thought the worse. It had to be important. I went the room of a friend to use his phone. As I dialed the number, I was bracing for the worst. My friend stood by as support.

"Hello."

"Yes, hey this is David. You said to call you."

"What did you do with the money?"

"What are you talking about? What money?

"Yeah, I got a call from the pastor. He said he was concerned because he hadn't received any of my tithes and offerings for the past six months when I was there. What did you do with the money?"

That was how my stepdad chose to respond to my call. Not asking how I was doing of if I needed anything? Should I have expected anything more? He hadn't called me during the two years I was on campus; not to check on me, ask about my grades, or how my life in general was going...nothing. Now, I thought it wasn't the reason he called me. First, I didn't steal any money from the church. My stepfather worked on most Sundays and gave me his tithes and offerings to turn in. I didn't take any of his money nor understand why the church misspoke and wasn't able to account for six months of his contributions. Further, was it the church's practice to call and question about tithes and offerings to lay members? I was outraged. The church had a perpetual building fund, and no building was built. Something was always happening, and the process of procuring the building was stalled. But the pastor and wife had matching expensive vehicles and lived in luxury apartments.

"I never stole any money! I always put it in the basket during offering time. When did they say it was missing?

"They said they haven't received any tithes from me since May of last year, which totaled over 8,000 dollars that you stole."

"I never stole no money from the church."

"You are coming home and getting a job and you gone pay back every cent you stole! I hate liars and thieves. And you are not 'bout to shame me in front of those people at the church! You can finish this semester but right after that you come home and pay back this money!"

He hung up the phone. I couldn't argue with him. His mind was made up before he called. He didn't have a question. It was only to inform me that I had to pay back the money to the church I hadn't taken. Because I couldn't prove it, my word was against theirs, and there was no way he was going to believe me before a pastor. As soon as the semester was over, I was to come home and work to repay what I didn't steal. I sat up in bed. My heart was racing. I felt the same anger I did the night I ended the call. I was plagued with pain because of the traumatic event until I paid the money. I was devastated. I blamed the church for the false accusation. I wasn't fully sure who was responsible, but somebody should've said something or double-checked. I went to my desk and began to type the memory...

Twenty-three

MY FIRST ASSIGNMENT

I returned to Milwaukee and continued at the same church. On Sundays, I reported for duty. One Sunday my cousin, who was the minister of music at his parents' church, invited me to help the choir sing at his church. I agreed. As I walked to the door, someone ran out. I thought it was weird but entered the small quaint church anyway. I thought I arrived in the Twilight Zone. The 100-seat church was in the ghetto or hood, classified as a storefront. Approximately 50 to 60 people were there for worship service. My cousin was playing the keyboard, which he turned up to its highest level of decibel. It was plugged into a monitor. A missionary was working on the microphone screaming, "Hallelujah" and "Thank you Jesus," to the top of her lungs. The windows were open. The only cooling systems were the oscillating fans set on full-blast and fan-waving congregants. The people were crying and worshipping, intoxicated with the glory I remembered. I felt desperately lonely. I kept my vow. I didn't want God around, yet I longed to *feel* him again. The mist of the anointing was thick. I knew most of the congregation. We grew up together in another church. I hadn't seen some of them in years. They looked different.

I thought I missed the service and got there in time for the altar call. I was sure I was told the time, and shouldn't have been that late, but I was. I fought my feelings and found a seat near the back. After they calmed down, a young lady went to the microphone and opened the testimony service. Growing up in the Pentecostal church, I was used to testimony service, but was under the understanding that we had progressed past it. We had those for Friday night, if at all. I was also concerned about altar call being at the beginning of service. I took a seat next to my cousin Jackie. Just then a woman stood to testify.

"Giving honor to God...shamado menae eshatalogi."

I looked up and noticed she started speaking in tongues.

"Giving honor to God...Ecakasee maoh dinat..."

She seemed to not be able to control herself. I thought she should have stayed seated until she was ready to speak in English. To my surprise, she was now intrepidly in tongues, yet I heard David being said.

"Radishiki my biotek DAVID....onfo inro rrustic David."

As she continued, her utterances were stronger and louder. My aunt, who was the first lady, was in a swivel chair in front of her. She turned her chair to face the woman. After she heard her call my name several times, she turned her chair toward me and held her arms out.

"David, come."

I was unsure if I was the only David in the room. I sat in complete disbelief and awe. What was happening? I thought I was in a dream. My cousin Jackie hit my leg and told me to get up. I was in a trance-like state. I slowly arose and cautiously went down the short aisle. What was about a seven-second walk seemed like 22 and one-half years long to go down. As I was approaching the front pew, the lady who was speaking in tongues walked to meet me and was in full throttle. Before she could say anything to me, I felt an unbearable pain, as if someone hit me with all their might in my abdomen. As my tears streamed down my face, I was unable to regain composure.

"God said He wants a yes."

The lady spoke in English. Immediately, with all that was in me, I stood up in direct defiance. Not again! I was sure I made myself clear when I told Him we weren't doing any yeses around here. Did He think I forgot or at least changed my mind? Well, I hadn't. I meant what I said!

I propped up, shook my head, vehemently insolent, and said, "No!"

Just as sure as I felt the pain which caused me to double over the first time, it returned with twice the impact, knocking me directly to the floor. I was in awe. I don't fall out. What was happening? Who were those people and why were they bothering me? I simply came to help this little choir with their song selections of the day. I was outraged and I wasn't going to stand for it. But it was too late. I was on the floor and the battle was on.

For the span of about three hours, I went back and forth with the altar workers who were trying to persuade me to accept God. I wasn't going to let them win. They took turns and were relentless. Even when I tried to act like I told Him yes, I hadn't. Several more demons were lying in wait. After the third hour, I was tired and went internal, while still rolling on the floor, to have a meeting. I told the remaining demons that the people weren't giving up and the only way I could end it was to release them and allow them to come back after I left the service. The demons quickly obliged, and they were off. I felt the difference after they were gone. I had a peace I hadn't felt in a long time. I was freed from every care in the world, yet I contemplated whether I would let them back. Oh, I did....

After that incident, I believed God tried to punk me into serving Him after I explicitly told Him I didn't want to. I thought He was a gentleman who wouldn't force himself on anyone. Well, what do you call that? I was furious and enraged.

"I'll fix and show Him."

I decided not to keep the demons I had but would search high and low for the best, strongest, and wickedest ones I could find. To do so, I had to recall and apply some of the tricks and practices I had done for years. I projected overseas, conducted interviews, and asked the demons to show me their powers before I granted access to them. I was on the prowl for the best of the best.

While at my other church one Sunday, after singing in the choir, the Holy Spirit was prevalent in the church. I heard the spirit of the Lord tell me to go to my cousins' church. I immediately resisted. I knew it was a setup. I heard it repeatedly, and I refused to accept the instruction. Then the Holy Spirit knocked me to my knees before the whole church. I was embarrassed. It was during praise, so I'm sure they didn't see me.

"I don't want to go there, and why are you speaking to me?

I was knocked on my face and began to roll. I knew then it was going to be a problem if I didn't submit. I quickly agreed and was released from the floor. I grabbed my things and went to their service.

Later that evening I received a visitation from a demon. He had an assignment from his master.

"You are to join that church you were at earlier today and tear it apart. They have been a nuisance to hell and must be stopped."

I was confused. What did that mean? How was it possible both God and the demons wanted me to do the same thing? I didn't learn until later that only God is omnipresent and omniscient. The demons had no idea God ordered me to go to the church. But why would they want me to tear up a church? I was told the pastor wasn't competent and unworthy of preaching. Because of my disdain for preachers, they knew I would be willing to take down any preacher that wasn't up to par. I wasn't sure if I wanted to go through with it. After all, that was the same church where I was in so much trouble a couple of months prior. I awakened from the memory and had no words. While shaking my head, I typed...

Twenty-four

OH, WHAT A NIGHT!

Friday nights were a highlight of our week. As in most traditional Church of God in Christ churches, we had deliverance or praise service every Friday. The service, as noted in Pentecostal church history, was a time for the saints to come together, fellowship in prayer, praise, share testimonies, and glean strength from one another. If anyone sought the Holy Ghost, it was an optimum time to have a tarrying service. Such was the case with the church I was assigned to tear apart.

On a particular Friday night, I was on the drums. I grew up in the church and learned how to do most of everything. As the service wore on and on, a young man in the audience who was about seventeen stood and testified that he wanted to be saved. The saints immediately started rejoicing, seeing it as a home run, and turned into a tarrying service. They ushered the young man to the altar. They believed in tarrying until someone confessed, gotten saved, and filled with the Holy Spirit.

"Save me, Jesus. Save me, Jesus. Save me Jesus," the young man rang out.

The stream of words soon filled into a river and quickly mounted into an ocean of chant and overflowed the church.

One could feel the Holy Spirit change the atmosphere, and as he submitted, the change metamorphosing in him was evident. The session went on for a few hours from eight o'clock until 10:00. My younger cousin who was around the same age as the teen fell asleep in the back of the church as they were in process of tarrying. I saw my aunt, the pastor's wife, go back and awaken him and told him to go to the altar and help them to tarry with the young man. I thought it was the funniest thing ever.

How did she think waking someone in the middle of their sleep would benefit tarrying? Was it because they were around the same age, and she believed the teen would turn over better if he had someone in his age bracket working with him? Did she think her son, after being awakened from slumber, would be in the mood to tarry with him? My cousin had questions too. I was tickled and threw my head back in laughter. I'm not sure if my aunt saw me or heard me laughing. She marched over to me too.

"You're laughing, but you need to be on this altar too."

I was taken off guard.

"No, I don't! Just worry about who you have up there now."

Under normal circumstances, I wouldn't have said those words. Even if I felt it, I would have just looked and kept quiet or gave a grimacing smile. She looked at me and marched away, seemingly unmoved.

"Mr. David, come here please."

I looked up. The pastor called me up for prayer. I sat in amazement. I knew she didn't tell him anything because I was watching, and she just left from in front of me.

"Mr. David. Come here please."

He repeated it with a smirk. I didn't want to go up there, but I knew I would seem disobedient or possessed, and then it would've become a problem. I quickly surveyed my many demons to make sure they were intact. Surely, I didn't want the same thing to happen as it did a couple of months back. I got up and moved through the crowd. Most of them were working on the young man. I figured it wouldn't have been so bad since their attention was devoted to him. I wanted to simply get through the prayer and move around back to the drums. I finally reached the front of the altar, and the pastor put his hand on me. I raised my hands and bowed my head. It was the standard prayer reception position. The demons inside were braced, and I had great confidence in them. I believed *we* would be fine. I heard the pastor praying in tongues, and I countered with my tongues. I also began to use the regimen of the imagery of receptivity to the prayer. My goal was to allow the pastor to feel he succeeded in his prayer and that I had received of the Lord.

All was going well, and I could tell he was winding down in the prayer. Just as I was supposing it to be ending, I felt his hand lift from the top of my head and back down. Hmm okay, what was that about? He lifted it again and another hand lay on my head, but something changed. It felt different, and I was severely uncomfortable. I lifted my head and slightly opened one eye, just enough to see that it was no longer the pastor praying but the lady I curtly spoke to. Where did she come from and why was she there? It wasn't expected nor wanted. I was glad I did my homework and gathered the necessary demons to handle the impact of the woman and her anointing. She began to pray, and I could feel the spirit of the Lord mounting and intensifying in an embrace. My demons became extremely uneasy. What was she doing and when would she stop? The war was on! I remained intact and unmoved for as long as I could, however, I didn't understand what was going on inside. While I felt much stronger than the first time I was confronted, I still sensed impending danger. She was in those tongues again, and I just wanted to bash her in her mouth to make her stop.

She was relentless, and I was wondering how much more of it I could take. Then, I heard her voice in the microphone in those same tongues. My nerves grew alarmed. I thought about causing the system to shut down, but I was sure they could see that I was the source. I thought to wait it out. After what seemed an eternity in tongues, she went into a Jesus chant, which almost caused all the demons to go into a chaotic mode. I tried to calm them and keep them intact, but it was becoming a daunting situation. Without warning, the most tragic thing happened. She called out one of my main demons and started rebuking it. I seethed with anger. How did she know to do that?

In building my inner kingdom of demons, I strategically placed demons in proper places for easy access and stable security. I had thousands upon thousands of demons that stayed in and around me for purposes of use. I braced myself in thought and mind that what she was doing wouldn't work. It was against my will, and I frankly wasn't going to have it. She told the church to unify themselves for the immensely powerful demon they were coming against. The congregants began the blood of Jesus chant. Now, I grew up in a sanctified church and knew when the church chanted, something was going to happen. To be honest, I was still cocky and refused to think there was a slight chance of breaking down my most formidable demon. After talking about the importance of becoming one in spirit and challenging my demon, she turned back to me and called the demon by its name, rebuked it, and told it to come out. I was astonished. How did she know the exact name of the demon? It wasn't a type of demon like the lying demon, stealing demon, or even a demon of witchcraft, but she identified the precise one. I was outdone! Something was going on internally.

The demon she called out broke and the other ones were in a tizzy. That was a vital and pivotal moment in my history, and the day and moment is forever written upon the tablet of my heart. I went internally and had an emergency conference. Where were some of the other demons that were under the rule of the mainstay demon? They evacuated when they saw their leader break. I thought they were stronger than God. In fact, I was not giving my will to Him to come in and deliver. I didn't ask Him to save me. I hadn't wanted Him around me. I thought hell and I had a pact, I was told that wouldn't be able to happen with the demons I searched high and low for, some across seas and on foreign lands. I thought I would be able to complete my tasks of tearing down churches and more focal preachers. I was assured God wouldn't be able to penetrate beyond those demons. I was cajoled to believe God was powerful, but not all-powerful.

What happened? Why did the plan fail after the prayers of just a few dozen measly congregants on a Friday night? I was confused. Just two years prior, I was convinced God wasn't the strongest, and the enemy was still able to do what he wanted to God's children and to those who were true to him. As I was having those thoughts, I was made aware of more demons evacuating as the saints were continuing nonstop and at full throttle of chant. I was panicked. The demons inside were trying to get me to calm down. I made a terrible mistake, was duped. I was a victim of my own will and taken captive to the enemy's side and didn't know how I got so far into it that I was willing to tear down God's kingdom. Tears of sorrow were pouring down my face.

The lady hushed the church and lifted my head to look directly into my eyes.

"You will die tonight."

I winced upon hearing those words.

"I am not talking to you, but I am talking to *you*.

I now understand what she meant. She wasn't speaking to the exterior man David. She spoke to the demon.

"You are all broken up, your legs are in his shoulders, and your head shifted to his stomach, and the reason he is even on his feet is that your elbow is holding him in his back. Oh, but you're coming out tonight. Y'all may have tricked me the last time, but you won't do it again."

She took the oil and began to pour it on my light olive-green silk shirt. They recommenced the chant. I was woozy because I was a part of something I didn't know how to get out of. While she spoke, she looked at me again. With the microphone in her hand, she asked me if I wanted to be clean, saved, and freed from the evil spirit. I had no choice but to say yes. I was embarrassed and didn't know what to do. I was completely disheveled. Then she stated I needed to denounce the demon and tell it that I no longer wanted it to dwell within me.

She said repeat after me.

"Devil..."

"Devil, I no longer want you in my life and I evict you out of my life and thus my body. I denounce your right to me for I am now the property of God."

I flinched as I spoke, and it was a struggle to get some of the verbiages out.

"Oh no, the devil is a lie," she pronounced and then put the microphone to my mouth and told me to repeat it.

"Devil..."

"Devil..."

She amplified her voice in the speakers and it echoed in the depths of my bones, which made me uncomfortable. I tried to back away because of my discomfort, but my aunt was behind me and held me steadfast.

"I no longer want you in my life and I evict you out of my life and thus my body. I denounce..."

Boom! I hit the floor. They continued working with me for most of the session. I don't remember much, but I was trying to clear up the mystery of which was to be trusted. I was outdone with being lied to and half-conscious about what was going on around me. My aunt and the lady stood over me.

"Look do you see how powerful it is," she said to my aunt in an almost admirable voice.

"Yes, we are going to have to do some extra fasting to get this out."

"But where did he get them from. They are not from here."

"I don't know, but what I do know is God can remove anything, and this is coming out," my aunt emphatically declared.

The session last from 10 at night until 4:00 in the morning. They got me up from the floor. I felt drained and mentally disoriented. I sat down in my seat, and the pastor got up to say some encouraging words to me. He asked the lady to share her testimony. She was the last person I wanted to hear anything else from. She had done enough. I just wanted to go home. She slowly stood up and took the microphone from the pastor.

"God says that was your last chance. He said he has cut you off. You are going to walk-out and a truck is going to run you over as you cross the street. Because you have rejected God, He has rejected you!"

After she revealed her prophecy, a woman in the audience started sobbing. Others hung their head. The room was still. I wasn't about to take a minute more.

"What do you mean this was my last chance?"

I no longer had a reason to hold my peace.

"I did everything you all told me to do! What more could I do? You said put your hands up, and that's what I did. You said say Jesus over and over, and I did that! You said turn around and repeat after you, and that's what I did. How is this my fault? How is it fair you couldn't cast out this demon?

"This is not a plea and bargain!"

"I'm not trying to have a plea or bargain. I'm stating the facts. How is it possible? I did everything you said to do, and because it didn't work, now I have to die!?

I was tired, worn, and beaten. I had been rolling around for hours and was ready for it to be over.

"Well, you best seek God!"

She slowly backed back to her seat. I couldn't believe that was all she had to say! The pastor took the mic and dismissed the service. I woke up with a burning sensation. The memory was more emotional than the others. I felt like I could literally have a heart attack. I walked over to the computer and typed...

Twenty-five

THE MORNING AFTER

Although the morning after wasn't an extraordinary event, the days that followed proved to be more drastic than the five to six-hour tarrying service. I went to my room in my home and didn't know what to expect or how to handle my life. I no longer felt comfortable at home, in my room, or anywhere else for that matter. Unexpectedly, a group of about six to eight witches began to taunt and torture me, day and night. As I walked, the witches flew over my head in a circular motion, screaming and howling without end. It was a maddening situation. God gave me grace and allowed me to understand that music was especially important. To combat the taunting of the witches, I bought the biggest and loudest headphones I could and continued to blast gospel music.

During that time, God blessed me to work at a prestigious corporation. My job was simply to take the requests sent down to the micro-fiche department via computer, find the discs, and send them through a type of vacuum system to the requesting department. It was a pure blessing because no one bothered me. I played music from the time I awakened until I went to sleep. I learned that not every gospel artist or song had the same effect on the demons. Some were unmoved when I played a CD, there was no impact on them. Being under the umbrella of Gospel music wasn't enough. I wondered what was more formidable than just words or a nice melody. While riding the bus, I kept my Bible open and consumed the word of God. My room also was a battleground. At night as I prayed, I was pushed around my room. I quickly learned how to pad my room so that I wouldn't get hurt during an attack. I was often pulled out of my bed and dragged across the floor. Sometimes the light was turned on for no reason. I was afraid, ashamed, and embarrassed to tell anyone about what was happening. I was unsure if somebody would believe me. I didn't want to feel more like a freak of some sort, especially since I already felt like one.

I awakened in a panic. It wasn't a particular dream, not a single event. Rather, it was a series of daily torture since the night after the Friday deliverance service. I could still feel the perpetual fear. I was nearly paralyzed by my fears. I knew I shouldn't be fearful, but I couldn't imagine what I had gotten into. I was sorrowful and confused. That night, I was sent a reminder of that time. I stumbled over to the computer and typed. I didn't write in a flow, but rather in stanzas. I struggled with writing the memory and how I felt. I just kept typing until it took form.

Twenty-six

DAILY ENCHANTMENT

I was still living with my stepfather while he was going through a divorce from my mother. I hadn't gotten over my negative feelings toward him. I later found out through my mother that he was trying to have my sister, who was diagnosed as mildly autistic, to have a full hysterectomy. I was appalled because she was only 10 years old. I knew he was a tad ashamed of her because of her condition. I understood the want to have a child that was like everyone else. At the same time, I knew it was his responsibility to care for and love her just as he would any other child. He also spoke of institutionalizing her. This was an outrage, and the doctors that consulted with him informed him she wasn't severe enough to institutionalize her. He then asked for her to be put on a drugged patch. It resulted in tremendous weight gain and numerous mood swings, which were frustrating for my sister and mom. My stepfather was fighting against paying child support for my sister. I only knew of him to be one who lived up to his responsibilities and always took care of his child. Whatever the reason, I heard all I was going to hear. I, in my heart, am a momma's boy. Although the relationship with my mom was dysfunctional, I couldn't stand for any more of this.

I began to work an incantation on my stepfather. I carefully planned it out. I wanted him to suffer like he made us suffer all those years. I didn't want it to be quick and short-lived. I wanted it to be payment for the fifteen years of pain in my life, seventeen years of heartache to my mother, and for what he continuously put my sister and brother through. Every day, I did an untraceable incantation that would cause a medical condition. Little by little, I wanted the pain to bend him over just as he bent the moral and integrity of the family. Progressively, I wanted discoloration to shame his face just as he had shamed us. I thought little about the repercussions of doing such an act. I also didn't think it wasn't the will of God, and I was acting out of the demonic realm.

One day I went to church and while waiting for my ride to take me home, Cordelia came to me.

"How are you doing?"

"Fine," I admitted as casually as I felt.

"Is everything alright?"

"No, I am doing fine."

"Oh, are the demons giving you any problems?"

"Umm, not any in particular. Is there something you saw or know about?"

I started feeling irritated.

"Well, are you dabbling in any occult practices?"

"No! Why would I do that?"

I didn't think about the incantations I did every day.

"Umm, no incantations to your stepfather?"

My countenance changed as I realized what I was doing. It was natural and almost second nature. I didn't wholly comprehend that what I was doing was against what God wanted. More than that, I had no desire to stop. I felt he earned what he was getting. They weren't there when he tortured us. He often came in the house at two or three o'clock in the morning and woke us up so that he could see us do work. He wasn't going to raise lazy children. To ensure we did chores or work every day, he wanted to witness us doing the work. It didn't matter that the house was already spotless. Since my mother was as a homemaker, she took impeccable care of the house. They weren't there to witness the horrible mental anguish he did to reduce my mother's morale and integrity as a wife, woman, and human. They had no clue about the degradation he caused to my manhood, self-esteem, and humanity. Not only had he continued to pursue foolishness with my mom and sister, God did nothing in seventeen years but allow his destruction. I was going to settle the score and right the wrong.

They told me I couldn't do anything but allow it to happen God's way. I wasn't ready or willing to hear it, but I knew I couldn't play both sides of the fence. I had to choose. Normally, I did either or, but it was a matter of making a choice and sticking to it. I decided to do it God's way but was unsure if I could abstain from witchery against my stepdad while still looking at him. God had a ram in the bush. My cousin Jackie graciously allowed me to stay at her house while I was going through my cleansing and deliverance session. During that time, I went from having everything I wanted, as far as material things, to having nothing. My clothes, for one reason or another, were unwearable. I had three pairs of pants and a handful of shirts. My shoes were run down. I didn't have a job. It was during that time when God was trying to develop a character of trust and dependence on Him. It was said that God didn't take us around the storm, nor did He deliver us from ever going through tests and fiery darts from the enemy. Rather, He develops our trust and dependence on Him during the storm. While going through is when we come to know Him. Like the Apostle, Paul said, "It was good that I was afflicted, that I may know Him in the fellowship of His suffering," (Psalm 119:71). I found this to be true. I was forced to lean and depend on Jesus and take Him at His word. Countless times, when I walked down the street, I was attacked by the unseen. I always tried to find a way of not looking conspicuous while calling on the strong name of Jesus. I've had things just come up missing while I was at work and didn't know how to explain where it was located.

I sat up in the bed, just as my regular routine. However, I was filled with mixed emotions and was alarmed by my memories. I realized just how deep my hatred for my stepfather ran. I was blinded by my rage and vengefulness and was practicing occultism every day. I comingled it with my love for God. I went over to my computer and with tears running down my face, I typed...

Twenty-seven

ANGELS FOLLOWING ME

One day I was at home and received a call from a friend's mom. She was frantic! She was crying and asked me to quickly come over because her son was in trouble. I asked what happened?

"Kevin was playing on his keyboard and singing songs to the Lord in worship when I heard him yell. I ran down the steps to find out what was going on. When I found him, he was at the keyboard but was red, shaking, and crying. I ran to him and questioned him. He said he didn't know but couldn't move. He can't move David...I am scared."

I told her I was on my way. I got my things and headed right over. As I was walking up to her walkway, it occurred to me that I hadn't prayed about what was going on and how the Lord wanted me to handle it. I knew better than to just go out on my own, yet in the state of urgency, I didn't realize what I was doing. I hurriedly prayed. I wondered if that was exactly what the devil wanted me to do as a setup, if it was something I wasn't prepared to handle, or if there could be repercussions.

"Please forgive me for acting out of impulse and not on clear instructions from you Lord. I don't know what is going on. You are God, strong and mighty, and you know if this is a trap. I trust in the gifts you have given me. But I don't know what I am about to face. What I need from you is to send me two angels, two of your finest please."

These were my exact words. I wanted them to be there with me to protect, guide, and shield me from any attack of the enemy should it have been a trap.

"I thank you that you hear me, and it is so in Jesus' name," I prayed.

I walked into the house and went downstairs. Kevin was moving about and appeared to be doing fine. I asked about what happened, and he told me he was singing songs to the Lord in worship and suddenly, out of nowhere, a force grabbed him, and he couldn't move. The more he tried, the stronger the force held him. He said he called out to his mother, and she came to him and started to panic. They prayed and prayed but nothing seemed to work. His mom decided to call me and went to the phone. Kevin remembered me telling him that even if all he had left was his voice, it was all he needed to overcome the devil by vocally calling on Jesus. That's what he did. He kept calling on Jesus, and the demon left as quickly as it came. He and his mom embraced each other and forgot I was on the way.

I was appreciative and relieved that everything was fine. I walked up the steps and when I entered the kitchen where his mom was washing dishes, I spoke, and she spoke back to me but mid-sentence she stopped. In slow motion, she turned her face toward me. I looked at her eyes, which were bulging, and she appeared to be stunned. She looked past me. I turned to see what was behind me. Nothing...I saw nothing but a window. I turned back to her and asked what the problem was. Still, in amazement, she pointed up and past me.

"Where did you get those angels from. They are the biggest ones I have ever seen!"

I laughed. I forgot I requested them.

"How many do you see."

"Two! And they are huge."

I told her I asked for them. I then wept. Out of the goodness of God, He heard and answered me, even when I hastily acted without consulting him.

That morning, I awakened from my dream. I wasn't panicked or anxious. I felt fine. I was relieved that I had a good memory. I waltzed to the computer and began to type...

Twenty-eight

WHAT'S YOUR JOB?

I had a dream, and in the dream, a group of us were walking along the road. We just left a convention. As we walked the streets on our way to the hotel, another group of people walked toward us. We could tell they weren't from the convention. As we neared, I noticed they were a group of Wiccans. I knew something was up. I started to calm myself and prepare for whatever was about to ensue. When we crossed paths, one of the men looked at me and we both stopped in our tracks.

"Whose side are you on?"

I was not expecting the question and in truth, it took me aback. I immediately knew my answer, either way, could cause difficulty. Before I could evaluate my decision, I responded.

"For Jehovah God, I live and will die!"

With those words, the man backed up and I knew it was on. He moved a great deal away and begins to charge toward me. I didn't know what to do, so I just stood there. When he was in arms reach, he lifted his nearest hand and brought it down toward my head. In response, I lifted my hand to block and cover the strike. When our hands collided, I was nearly overcome by the strength permeating from his hands. But God was my stay. Immediately the scene changed, and we were at the foot of my steps of my house. I had holy oil in my hand and was slinging it at him as I rebuked him in the name of Jesus. He was flinching as we continued up my steps. I discovered what I was slinging wasn't oil but water. I stopped.

"How dare you enter my house for battle? Get out!"

He looked me in my eye and said, "I'll see you again."

I woke up.

A few months later, I walked into my new place of employment. The manager, as a normal custom, took me on a tour of the office and introduced me to my peer workers. As I walked to the last room, my spirit started to wreak havoc within me. I ignored the feeling and moved on. I stood in the middle of the room with everyone's back to me as they worked. The manager gave a brief overview of the room and asked everyone to welcome me. When they turned around it was the group from my dream. The lead of the team was the man who attacked me. What a welcome.

I soon had many battles and came to know God and His principles from that house. Every day before I went to work, I prayed and asked God to cover me in the blood. I didn't know what would happen and I silently rebuked the enemy. One day while at work, I went to the bathroom. I closed the door and locked it. Boom! As I turned around, I felt as if someone had taken a crane with a demolition ball on it and hit me in my chest with it. My whole body went numb. Everything happened in slow motion. I felt my body slide down the wall. I didn't have a chance to grasp what was going on.

"Ha, I got you now!"

I immediately found strength and spiritual indignation and rebuked him as I stood on my feet. After I finished with the demon, I staggered to the stall. While I was trying to gain my composure, I was notified that more demons were on their way to attack me. I instantly consulted God to find out what to do.

"Go to the mirror and rebuke the witch that is sending them."

The spirit of the Lord resonated in the pit of my spirit. I immediately went into a debate with God. I knew the world of witchcraft and its laws and principles. Mirrors were a credible source of portals of passage. I only knew of sending messages and transmittals in that method and was hesitant to use it under the Spirit's instruction. I recognized the unction was from God, but it felt familiar to my former life and training. I second-guessed that method. I only had a few moments and less than that to do something. I re-asked the question.

"Go to the mirror and rebuke the witch that is sending them."

I was reassured and felt at peace. It was the spirit of the Lord telling me to do so. I followed the instructions and found solace and tranquility...until the next time.

I sat straight up and was shaking. I nearly stumbled to my computer. I remembered the emotions and spiritual throws of those type of battles. I typed...

Twenty-nine

PRAY FOR THE CHURCH

O ne day, as I was sitting at my desk at work I began to cry. "Lord why is this happening to us. Why are you allowing this to go on and how much longer will it be?"

It had been a couple of years since I prayed at the church and the Lord told me to get pen and paper to write out what He said regarding the state of the church. I thought the conversation with the pastor and his wife would be a turning point. I was sure the intervention would be the beacon of light to guide him, as we are all human and need to be guided. However, it wasn't what seemed to happen. The church was steadily going downhill. I was a concerned associate elder, deflated, and overwhelmed. It was hard to sit through church services. I took a job that allowed me to work on Sundays so that I didn't have to go to church. But I couldn't help but wonder what was going on.

The members were emptying the seats and the leaders would just say, "God was purging the church." Well, who's going to be left to purge if they all leave?

"Get your Bible!" the spirit spoke out.

I picked up my Bible and opened it.

"For the pastors are become brutish, and have not sought the Lord: therefore, they shall not prosper, and all their flocks shall be scattered" (Jeremiah 10:21).

I was devastated. The pastor is brutish? I thought brutish was a caveman type of person or a tyrant who was brutal and didn't care about the feelings of others. That was not my pastor. I started to become offended. How could God say something so slanderous against my pastor? I lived with him, and I knew he is a humble man. Yes, he had his flaws, but don't we all. Also, where does God get off being mean and crude? God said nothing else. I was sure upset with the Lord. I kept turning the Scripture in my mind. Why is God saying this? I could see the ending, which stated, "...and all their flocks shall be scattered," but I couldn't see the beginning. I went straight home from work, went into my room, and closed the door.

"Get your Commentary."

I did as commanded, and I knew just what the Lord wanted. When I looked up the passage it wasn't what I imagined. Brutish in fact meant that the pastor was dull hearted and wasn't seeking the Lord's guidance over his flock. After I read it, He began to pour out His concern and disturbance regarding the pastor. After sobbing and lamenting over what God said to me, I walked out of my room.

I found my aunt and told her what happened. We began to share the sentiments of our heart concerning the pastor and the church. I admired her inner strength and determination to keep her head above water. With her transparency, she showed her humanity and dire need of the Lord's help. As we were speaking, the pastor came in and heard us in the kitchen. He came in and took a seat. It was quite the setup. He was trying to hear and be nosey, not realizing we were speaking about him. As we continued, I asked why he didn't do what God asked of him.

"I don't know, but since he's sitting here, just ask him."

She whisked out of the kitchen to prepare for a service. The pastor and I just looked at each other. I won't forget the look on his face as he wondered what he stumbled into. I began from the top and told him what happened. The last time I had a talk with him regarding what God said, he seemed receptive. However, according to God, he hadn't done anything about it. I told him what God had said from the Scripture. He became more than defensive and outright told me I was incorrect, and he had been seeking God. I was flabbergasted. I didn't make it up nor was God incorrect. The pastor's posture indicated full revolt against what was being said. I was thrown off guard and had to regain my bearings. The pastor was playing victim. I argued in his defense and miserably lost. He believed I was trying to assassinate his character. But I didn't say it, so I wasn't able to retract it.

The pastor began to state his defense as if he was in the courtroom and wanted to cross-examine me as a witness. I let it go on for a minute then the prophet in me exploded. The Holy Spirit in me reminded him of all the times he was told to fast, and he didn't. He was to go to the church, shut himself away, and pray, yet he chose to sleep. The spirit began to run a litany of examples. In public and private settings, he yielded to the flesh rather than the spirit. As I was allowing the spirit to work, my aunt walked in and confirmed what was being said and left.

After a list and tally of recounting, I saw my pastor as I hadn't seen him before. He was sobbing and weeping. The Holy Spirit convicted his heart. I hoped it would start the process of improvement.

I jumped out of my bed and onto the floor. When I opened my eyes, I realized I was having another memory dream. I reclined on the floor, panted, and tried to calm down. I was full of mixed emotions. When I regained my strength, I got up and went over to the computer, turned it on, and typed...

Thirty

AM I READY FOR ORDINATION?

One day while riding with my pastor on an errand, he alerted me that Courtney and I would be taking the elder's ordination test in the upcoming State Holy Convocation Meeting. I almost choked. He told me that we proved to be ready for the next level. He listed many reasons, but I couldn't help but think why he was saying those things. I didn't see what led up to our selection. It was the worst time for me because I was at a place when my salvation was more unstable than ever. The ordination should have happened when I was much more solid in conviction and dedication to God. Could it have been that my pastor observed our maturity and knew that the hand of the Lord was ready to elevate me? I wasn't convinced, so I had to test the water.

I stopped him and asked if I had the opportunity to decline. The ordination wasn't an important occasion. Clearly, I wasn't big on being a preacher, and being an elder was not a glamorous position. If anything, it meant paying more dues and having more reports. As soon as I posed the question, he chimed that I could, but then he couldn't be blamed for holding us back. Who was us? That is when I knew he hadn't come up with it. Someone else was responsible. After a couple of conversations with others, I concluded that my belief was indeed true. Some people approached and accused him of holding Courtney and me back, and that was his remedy. Sigh. When I arose from the memory, I was wiping tears from my eyes. I could still feel the disappointment I felt knowing my pastor who I had served for several years and even lived in his house, had to be coerced into the decision. I typed...

Thirty-one

BRUTISH PASTORS

I received instruction from the Lord.

"Go to the church one hour before every service and pray." That wasn't what I wanted to do. It meant I had to leave work and go straight to the church to be on time to meet the Lord in prayer. Could not I just pray when I got there? Most of the time, the church was late anyway! I wanted to rest for a few minutes and debrief before running out to get to church. Was there no one else who could do this? Why me? What exactly am I praying for? Is it for the church? Is it for me?

I wrestled with the command for about two months. I surrendered and started going to the church one hour before the scheduled start time after a series of repercussions following my disobedience. I wasn't interested in going but I went anyway. At first, I got down on my knees, and like my traditional training, started with a hymn and then prayer. Since I didn't have a pre-described purpose to pray, I thanked Him and allowed the Holy Spirit to pray and followed its prompting.

What started as a hesitant time of prayer turned into me not being able to wait to get there and meet the Father in prayer. At times, the spirit led me into intercession for specific church members or others that were connected to the ministry. Other times, I stood in the gap and diverted the plan of the enemy that was after the leadership or lay leadership. I allowed God to minister to me as well, and that is when He revealed himself and me. I learned many things about God by spending time with Him and allowing Him to minister to me. During that time, I didn't talk. I just listened. Those were the most pivotal times for me to establish a quality relationship with the Father. From our relationship, I learned to hear the voice of the Father in a new way, how to yield to the tugging of God, and His principles of His love and patience. Those were the basic tools I needed to get me through the testing period, and I am grateful I yielded to His Spirit. I also learned that God always first showed me who I was.

Many times, when the saints got there, I was still in prayer. They joined me. Sometimes, the Holy Spirit dwelled so much that our prayer time became the service. I thank God for pastors that were willing to allow God to develop a character of prayer in me. One day, my pastor came to me and asked me to seek God during my prayer time regarding the church's growth and anything else He might say. I discerned a decline in the church's growth. What was increasing seemed to be decreasing. It is always said that God would clean house and anything that is in the way, He would remove. This is the reason some people had to leave. With each person who left, it was made to appear that they were unwilling to heed to the voice of the Lord or had allowed the enemy to fill their heart or blind their eye to the truth. Some former members also served on auxiliaries of the church. Those that departed were part of the following ministries:

- Sunday School Department
- YPWWYD
- Prayer and Bible Band
- Transportation Ministry
- Music Ministry
- Pastors Aid
- Mothers Board
- Purity
- Hospitality
- Men's Department
- YWCCWD
- Circle of Charity
- Sunshine Band

The church had a lot of opportunities to serve, which was a wonderful thing, however, having only twenty active members put a strain on the ministry. Each auxiliary group had a president, vice president, and workers. People were involved in several activities at once. Each auxiliary was responsible for meeting a monetary goal. To say the least, that type of structure proved to be strenuous at best and began to break down. People began to complain and point fingers. It seemed the church was under attack, and nothing was going well.

I knew what was happening and was fully aware of the struggle. Being young in the church, I wasn't as savvy and didn't have a lot of experience with *church work*. I grew up in a church that started the same way, and it grew to a prominent size. Because my family actively participated in the growth of the church of my youth, I was able to see some things up close and personal. Yet, what I learned wasn't enough to for me to get what I thought would be easy to replicate. After all, God has no respect for persons. When my pastor asked me to go before the Lord, I knew it was a legitimate request, however, I felt it wasn't my place to ask God about the church on the behalf of the pastor. I wondered why he didn't petition God. Hmm, he was the leader. He should've been speaking to God, not me for him. I decided not to seek God on his behalf.

A month later, even I was tired of the downward spiral. One evening while in prayer before service, I asked the Lord what was going on with the church. I no longer wanted to be blind about what was happening. I wanted to know for sure if it was a time of testing or pruning or if there was something I overlooked or had ignored. He immediately started speaking.

"Get up and get a pen and paper."

He said it as if He'd been waiting for me to ask.

"Get up and get a pen and paper!"

I should think not. I am on my face before the Lord God, and I shall not be moved.

"Get up and get a pen and paper."

Why was I hearing that? It was unlike Him to do so. It was counterproductive to what I was trying to accomplish. I was asking a question that was on my heart, and He directed me to get a pen and paper.

"Get up and get a pen and paper!"

His voice was more forceful and commanding. It clicked in my mind what was going on. The Lord was asking me to get a pen and paper because He wanted me to either write something specific or take notes while He spoke to me. I was embarrassed because it took me so long to get it. I was having a *blonde* moment in the Lord's presence. Who does that?

I retrieved pen and paper from my bag and went back to where I was and sat up, attentive to take notes on whatever He said. He began to share some things I believe I wasn't ready to receive. He shared that he gave explicit instructions to the pastor. He told him to feed His sheep and to be the covering according to his word. But something different was going on, and He was unhappy with it. Also, He didn't call the pastor's wife to pastor but only to uphold or be the helpmeet. Due to the pastor's lack of standing up and being the pastor, he had his wife to step up and shoulder much of the burden meant for him. The pastor's actions were reflected throughout the church, with each auxiliary, established board, and the governing agent.

God summoned me to do a quick inventory. As I thought of every component of the church, I realized what He was telling me was true. Each of the vice presidents were doing more work and more dependable than the presidents. Even when I was a vice-president of pastor's aide, I was doing much of the work. The president provided excuses as to why she couldn't get it together. She willingly resigned, said she couldn't do it, and wanted to swap with me. When we did, so did our spirits. I was quickly exhausted and just couldn't get it together. She was remarkably good and had all the energy and commitment in the world. How was it possible? Were we in a backward decline?

What were we to do next? I had many questions as God was continuing to speak to me about how the dysfunction and debauched system was unfolding, and the pastor was more interested in following his dreams of doing personal business than doing the Lord's business. God allowed the pastor to come off his job to have a full-time ministry, but he filled his days doing otherwise. I heard enough and was in a pool of tears. I put down the pen and just said, "Amen!" I was embarrassed. I wondered what it all meant and should be done. I took the pen and paper and put them in my bag, almost wanting to be awakened from a bad dream. I cried the entire service. I was unable to focus. I just wanted to get it out of my head, and that's what I did. I placed the notebook on my dresser, never to be seen again for about the space of one year.

One day, Cordelia from my church called me and started venting. She shared with me about her dismay with the pastor. Cordelia closely worked with the pastor and his wife. I knew she wouldn't purposely defame or speak against her leader. From her tone, I could tell she was upset. I listened to her go on and on for a while. I stopped her and requested the story from the top. The pastor came to her and asked her to pray about the church and why it was declining because there was no progress in sight. She went on a fast and prayed for the church. Then the Lord spoke to her heart. The Lord is my witness. I wasn't prepared for what came next, although I should've seen the setup. She began to flow with what the Lord told me a year ago. As she spoke, her words began to ring in my ear and my memory was triggered. I went from downstairs to upstairs to look for the notepad.

"Do you know that cow got mad at me when I told him what the Lord said, like I made it up or was out to get him!"

I can only guess that Cordelia thought I wasn't paying attention because I was silent.

"Are you even listening to me?"

"Yes."

"Then, why aren't you responding?"

"Uhh..."

"Oh my God! He told you too?"

She was happy to know she accurately heard and had a witness.

"Did he act like that when you told him too?"

"Umm..."

"What? You mean you haven't said anything. You didn't tell him what God said. You...cow...you are bogus too!"

She was a tad flustered. That was the kind of relationship we had, which was quite tickling to say the least.

I told her if I could find the paper, I would tell them what I was told in prayer. She assured me I would find it and I had better tell them. I agreed and turned around. At the oddest place, I set my hand down and picked up a notepad and opened it. I wrote the words from the Lord on the night of prayer in that notepad. It was in my face. I had to live up to the promise. I eased downstairs and into their room. The pastor's wife was reading as she most often did. I peeped into the room, and she looked at me. I casually smiled, which always got me caught up. She laughed and told me to come in. I sat for a moment, wanting to disappear, wanting it not to be happening. She asked me what it was that I didn't want to say. I'm sure she sensed my tension and waited to see if I was about to burst. How would she take this? What would be her response? I hadn't told someone what I was about to say. I already was uncomfortable saying that God spoke anything. I felt unworthy of the right to do so. I also didn't want to say anything in my efforts or distort what the Father wanted to convey. I went ahead, and little by little, started from the beginning until the point when God started speaking.

"Well, are you going to tell me what He said or what?"

I took a deep breath and unfolded my notepad. I brought it with me so that I wouldn't miss anything. I told her everything that was written on the paper. As I spoke, I could feel her intensely looking at me, almost hanging on to every word coming out of my mouth. I ended and sheepishly looked at her. As she spoke, I sensed in her voice that a cry was on its way. About two months prior, God told her the same thing while she was away at a convention. She didn't mean to be out of place, but like many of us, she was trying to do what she saw was missing, and it was not the will of God. As she spoke, her tears began to form and fall down her face.

She showed such vulnerability. I hadn't noticed it before. She was the strong formidable force against Satan, the warrior who knew no defeat, looking as shamefacedly as the rest of us, the laity of the church. At that moment, something went through to the pit of my soul. I witnessed that not all preachers or authorities refused to be human. Even though I knew, and they would've agreed, they needed the Lord just like we did. It was okay to show their humanity. My life was changed in that moment. Still in my feelings, she told me not to be afraid to tell what God had said.

"Whoever He gives a word to about someone, always let them know or else the accountability would be on you."

She then asked the question I internally begged to not be asked.

"When did God tell you this?"

"Umm, about a year ago,"

I tried to speed through that process, but if you know my aunt, that wasn't going to work.

"What!"

For ten minutes, she let me have it. At least it was back to normal. I felt relieved, remorseful, but relieved.

"When are you telling pastor?"

My facial expression was revealing.

"When he comes back, you all will talk!"

I scurried out of there as quickly as my short legs allowed.

I was upstairs in my room for not nearly twenty minutes when I heard the voice of my pastor calling me from downstairs. I knew my aunt told him I had something to say. She knew I would wait as long as I could before confronting him. I went downstairs and told him all the Lord had given. He seemed to accept it. He nodded to indicate he understood. He asked when God told me.

"One year..."

"What took so long?"

"I was uncomfortable and didn't want to say what I heard the Father communicate."

He as well admonished me to always tell whatever the Lord gave because it was always needed and valuable.

"Besides, you don't want to get in trouble with God for being disobedient."

I was glad it was over.

Two days after I had the conversation with my pastor and his wife, I came home from work, and he was sitting on the couch in the living room watching television.

"Mr. David, let me ask you something."

He had a somber and inquisitive look on his face.

"When you said I was to do the Lord's work and not my own business, did you mean I couldn't have any business of my own?"

I couldn't believe what I was hearing.

"After two days, you now have a question. Furthermore, this question isn't for me. I didn't have any requests from you. The Lord did."

I sensed he was trying to find a loophole in what God wanted so that he could appease Him and his plan. I was immediately agitated. It was as if he was the member, and I was the pastor. I responded the way he often did when we the sheep tried to pull that on him as the under-shepherd.

"I don't have any words as to what He meant, but I'm sure since it's God's message, He won't mind telling you exactly what He meant. I encourage you to seek Him and see what He says."

I walked upstairs and prepared for service.

St. Emmanuel church held a city-wide reputation of being a church of power and mighty in deliverance. This was true, oh so true. I witnessed many demons cast out, and some things you would have only heard about in the olden days of church. It was nothing for a tarrying service to break out. It was commonplace for a demon to come in from the streets, and we stopped to deal with it. We didn't escort them out. If they had the nerve to come into our setting, they were foolish enough to challenge the Lord our God, and we had the gall to cast them out. A real conviction to the manifested power of God and His deliverance resulted. Many times, prophecy came forth and it didn't matter who it came through. It was unheard of to come to church and leave the same way. When I woke up from the memory...I shook my head and typed...

Thirty-two

PRAY FOR THE PASTOR

One day, the pastor's wife came to me and asked if I would partner with her in prayer for the pastor and church. She expressed her concerns, which matched my own. We decided to fast and pray together in the mornings before our day began for the pastor for seven days. The first day my aunt came to my door. I didn't feel like getting up, but because of my commitment and where else was I going to go, I got up. She said we would trade off leading the prayer in the mornings and she would start. I was happy to hear it because I didn't want to begin. We prayed for about an hour, but I was kind of disturbed about the way the prayer went. I always thought if we had a purpose in prayer, it would be the theme with everything we prayed for, focused on, meditated about, and read in Scriptures. It would only change as led by the Holy Spirit. When the pastor's wife prayed, she prayed a blanket prayer. It wasn't anything wrong per se, I thought she would've focused on the purpose, which was pastor. I thought it was just a casual regular prayer.

The next day as we began prayer, I did what I knew. I earnestly prayed for the pastor in every area my spirit and I could think about. I wanted the devil to know I was in an all-out war until God told me enough. I was coming for whatever it was he had set up against the pastor. I prayed until the first family brought their children to the daycare. My aunt simply got up and let them in. Shortly after she let them in and settled the children, she returned to prayer, and we concluded. We went on like that for about a week. A week to the day we started our fast and prayer, I received a call from Cordelia, which I missed. Jami, Cordelia's daughter, called to tell me they hospitalized the pastor. Long story short, he had bleeding on the brain. They also saw dried blood as well. They could only assume he suffered a concussion from the accident he had about a month prior. The doctors had to immediately perform surgery on him, and it was going to take a while before he was able to come to church or do any stimulating activities. At that time, there were only two preachers left from the original seven. It was decided that my God-brother Courtney and I would trade-off bringing the word of God. A month to the date he had his first surgery, they found more bleeding. He had to repeat surgery and the recovery period.

Courtney and I carried the church under the supervision and advisory of the pastor's wife. The church began to grow and strengthen during the period we prayed for our pastor. I believed when the pastor returned, he would be ready and equipped to charge ahead with the progress we made. Unfortunately, that was not the case. He seemed the same and proved it with actions—no signs of improvement whatsoever. The church was already incorporated and was interested in becoming 501(c)3, which would've allowed for greater opportunities to serve and make a stronger impact in our community. The church met with the lawyer, and he provided suggestions and sometimes directives, which were contrary to what the pastor wanted. For the church to secure the status of the non-profit with 501(c)3 status, it needed to have a board of directors. The lawyer also stated it would be a conflict of interest for the pastor to be on the board.

With limited options, the pastor wanted everyone on the board to be from inside the church. I had the pleasure of being selected. The pastor told me he wanted me to chair the board. I had some experience, but not in the chairing capacity. I gave him my list of reasons about why I wasn't qualified for the position. Of course, there was no way to refuse. It was settled. At the first meeting, the pastor set up the board and gave us our purpose and responsibilities. He also introduced me as the chairman of the board. The meeting was held in the presence of the pastor, and he stayed at the second meeting too. I was fine with him being there. I heard my aunt and Cordelia speaking about and questioning why the pastor needed to be present at the meetings without an invitation. Then, the pastor's wife pulled me to the side and asked how the board was coming along and how I felt about the pastor being at the meeting. I told her I didn't have a problem with him being there at all. As far I was concerned, he should've been there just to make sure I was comfortable and able to defer to him for any questions or concerns I couldn't answer. I thought he was being proactive by making sure the board would become solid and properly grow. She seemed confused. I couldn't quite grasp what it was about. Later that week, the pastor came to me and apologized for being at the meetings. I thought it was needless for him to do so and started to tell him it was fine with me. He told me Cordelia and his wife convinced him that he was wrong for doing so. He only came because he didn't know how I was going to run the board. In fact, he didn't have faith in me.

I didn't know how to take it. Since he convinced me to take the position in the first place, I thought he believed I was a match for the position. I determined he didn't agree with me being the chair, and I might have been recommended by his wife or Cordelia. It took them to show him that he was wrong and sent him to apologize. After I left the church, I found out the pastor went to one of the members of the board and said he had to watch out for me because he felt I might be trying to take over the church. When I was told, I was brokenhearted. I felt betrayed. How could he say such a thing? I lived in his house and faithfully served with all I had. If he didn't want to have me on the board or doing whatever for the church, he should have said something. I couldn't get over it. Why didn't he come to me with his concern? With everything I gave to the church, my tears, money, and time, why couldn't he, of all people, see it? I gave nearly all my twenties to the church and abandoned many amenities to support the work and vision he oversaw. Not once did I try to steal or usurp his authority. I didn't want to preach nor pastor a church. What was going on in his mind?

As I awakened, I could feel the pain of disappointment and betrayal. I didn't think the pastor intentionally set up to sabotage me, however, in his own *stuff*, he was mistrustful and side eying. I walked over to my computer, and I typed...

Thirty-three

THE MOVE

My aunt was sobbing when she came to me. I asked what was wrong, and she began to tell me. While she was cleaning the house, she found a letter from their landlord addressed to the pastor. She opened it and it read, "Per our conversation, your lease will expire on June 1, 2003." Because it was already mid-March, it seemed unbearable to her. They had no savings to use to prepare for the move. She went to the pastor.

"When did this happen?"

"I just received the information in the mail."

"But it says, 'Per our conversation....'"

"Yeah, I spoke to him last week. He informed me that we had to move."

"What are we to do?

In times past, he was consistently upfront and timely in his business, as well as supportive and personable. It was a breathtaking surprise.

The next day, my aunt saw the landlord and took the opportunity to confront him regarding the unexpected news. After exchanging pleasantries, she told him that she and her husband received the disturbing letter. He appeared to be confused.

"Don't you think it's a bit sudden and unfair of you to just now let us know we have to move?"

"What do you mean this was sudden?"

She told him what her husband shared with her. It wasn't the first time they spoke about it.

"Is this the first time you are hearing of this?"

"Yes."

"We had been speaking about this since last October."

Her mouth dropped. She was in utter disbelief.

"Are you serious?"

"Yes, I'm planning to expand the property to make a transitional living center for women. The pastor said it was okay. A plan is in motion, so it wouldn't be a problem to move out by June 1st."

She said it felt like a ton of bricks fell on her. Not only had she been misinformed, but they weren't a team. Her childcare business was run out of the church. She had to find another location. Why did he withhold the information from her? She could've understood it if he had held the information from the church at large, but they were supposed to be a team. It was unfair. When she went back to her husband and questioned him, he didn't disagree, but stated that he was waiting on God to send money for them to move.

As she completed the story, I felt a large lump in my throat. I had no answer for what happened. I didn't understand how the pastor believed God would drop money out of the sky without our active participation in the plan. The landlord said that he was sorry for the confusion and his hands were tied. He sought a grant to convert the church and succeeded. Because it was federal money, he had to follow their rules, which was that the place had to be void of occupancy to receive the grant dollars. We didn't have a say in the matter.

We called a board meeting to discuss our next steps. With our account near zero and no leads or thoughts as to where we could go, we had to start from nothing. The landlord was gracious enough to waive the rent for three months. We were heartbroken and felt betrayed. That was the church building of my conversion. We partook in many three-day shut-ins, tarrying, and deliverance services. We put a lot of work into the building, including replacing the carpet, installing tiles, and painting the walls. We held fundraisers, chicken, fish, ribs, soul food, and other dinners, fashion shows, walk-a-thons, the rainbow of colors, women in hats, 7-Up program, Bad women in the Bible, plays, and many dance productions. Was it all for naught? We had such an attachment to the place and hoped to grow and fill it and eventually move on, but it wasn't the way I anticipated. Every time I thought about it, my tears flowed. Almost unable to breathe, I sought God. What was he doing?

Many people already left the church. It was said over and over that God was pruning the place, and those who departed were unwilling to yield to God's will. I often thought of it and pondered its reality. Was everyone leaving because of their own will? Did they not want to be with God? I then received unexpected news. I was devastated. My cousin, who was the pastor's son and musician, left the church. I couldn't believe it! What did it mean? Anthony was my best friend since I could remember. We spent countless hours talking on the phone about everything. He was the reason I came to the church. Half of the church had the same testimony about him because of his influence in the community. Anthony played an intricate role in the church and in my personal life. He was one of the few people who dealt with me due to my supposed evilness. We sang in the same community choir where we were predominant fixtures. I genuinely loved my cousin, and we traveled together and looked out for each other. We were known to come as a package deal. When you saw one of us you saw the other. He was the little quiet one and I was the big loud one. Together we had seized towering forces and caused formidable securities to crumble. He was leaving me at his parent's church. I understand he did what he felt was best for him, but the selfish part of me couldn't understand why he thought it was a suitable time to do so. We understood each other musically and spiritually. We were the Clark Sisters' children. He was Dorinda's child, and I was Karen's child. How could he have done that to me? We were a team, and then he was gone. Who was going to play behind me or sing with me?

The following Sundays were some of the worst in my life. I cried and cried. Where was Anthony? Many others began to leave as well. We were one big family and spent nights and days with each other. Most of us were in our early twenties. We had much energy and spent it with each other. If we weren't traveling in a community choir, we were shopping or going to conventions or out of town. After church, we convened over the pastor's house to eat, fellowship, and play a Scrabble board game, the official St. Emmanuel Game. When one of us was hurting, we all hurt and went to see about each other. In a way, we had to have each other's back due to the rigidness of our parishioners. Many times, we ganged up on one another when one was trying to leave.

One time I left the church because of the inappropriate actions of the leaders. I had enough and was fuming about the way I was mistreated. The Sinclair sisters came to my job after I refused to answer phone calls. They advised me to get back to church. I flatly refused to listen to them. After I thanked them for coming, I marched to the back of the office. They followed me. I now understand that it was the work of God. My boss was already gone, so I was the only one to finish and lock up. They refused to leave until I broke down and complied. We formed a deep relationship with others at the church and nurtured each other. It was falling apart before my eyes.

After a lot of searching and looking, we decided to share churches with one of our fellowship churches in our jurisdiction. On the day of the move, I internally cried all day and had to escape to the bathroom to release my tears. Of course, as in every church, only a handful of what was left of the members came to help, which made the move more strenuous and tiring. I was beginning to spiritually flatline. I was praying and fasting with no results. It seemed as if God had forsaken us as a church, and I didn't know why. I lived with the pastor and wife and knew they loved God, so why was God doing that? We began services in the afternoon at the shared church. As they were finishing up their service, we prepared for ours. I refused to sit in the pulpit at the new church. In a way, I was being rebellious because the facility wasn't ours. I was grateful for the open door, but I didn't understand what was going on.

Thirty-four

IT WAS TIME!

Richard, one of my best friends who came to the church and had tremendously grown, informed me that he was leaving the church. I felt the pain all over again. How was I to continue like that? Again, I went to church in tears.

"Lord, this is ridiculous."

I sat up and shook my head. It was as if it was happening all over again. The memory was so lucid and felt real. I walked over to the computer to type.

I cried for St. Emmanuel! It just didn't seem fair. Where do I go?

It was time! I approached the end of my journey in Milwaukee. My soul knew it. Have you ever had a concrete knowing? There was no tangible evidence, but the knowing was conclusive. No persuasion was needed to understand its meaning. I didn't have a plan. I had no place to go. I was assured my time in Milwaukee had run its course.

I was working at Heartlove Place, a nonprofit organization. They connected communities through Christ to empower people, motivate families, and build stronger neighborhoods. Their mission was to integrate self-help, motivation, and empowerment, and provide physical and spiritual support. I was the executive administrator to the executive director. I witnessed the inner workings of the world of nonprofits and learned first-hand how to create contracts, build grant proposals, conduct fundraisers, and communicate with internal and external stakeholders. I was inspired to learn more and expand my leverage within the community.

The organization sat on Martin Luther King, Jr. Drive in what was considered the ghetto. We provided several programs that catered to the impoverished community. We provided youth and teen programs for ages 13-17 which were designed to incorporate our core developmental areas of spiritual, educational, physical, creative, and social growth. We filled a major gap in Central Milwaukee by offering the ProStart Culinary Arts Program. Participants were trained and prepared to obtain entry-level careers in the food service and hospitality industry. We also offered ServSafe Manager and Youth Employment training. In addition, HeartLove Place was an approved vendor of the Department of Public Instruction (DPI) and worked with the following food programs: Child and Adult Food Program, Summer Meal Service Program, and the Nutritional School Lunch Program. We provided catering services for banquets and business meetings.

Some of my most amazing memories are the times when people came off the street to seek help for food or clothing and the staff immediately assisted. It was the highlight of my day. It helped us to keep our perspectives in place. We can work for an organization that makes a difference, yet when not hands-on and directly involved with the community, we may feel the weight of our daily tasks and miss the immediate impact of our work. Working there inspired me to want to do more. My boss and I had several conversations about completing my degree. I attended several colleges and universities but didn't finish. It was crazy. I signed up for the classes I needed and completed my assignments with all A's, but near the end of the semester, I stopped going to class. I ended up dropping the courses. In Wisconsin, I enrolled in eight schools. I knew I needed to get my degree, but I was a part of many activities, and I didn't commit to concluding my education. I needed a change of scenery, somewhere where my activities were limited, and I could focus on my education.

As well, I felt stifled in all areas of my life, from church, school, family, and friends. I wanted to experience more, see more, do more, and know more. I believed moving would be mentally liberating, especially since I was in the same place all my life. Knowing life didn't have to be the same, I wanted to open my eyes to new experiences and relax my mind. I wanted to escape from the reality I thought I *had* to live. In our fast-paced world, it was hard to set everything aside and look at myself to find out if my life at the time was what I wanted. I thought if I moved away, I would be forced to answer. I was in a position to look at what I wanted to do career-wise and understand what made me. I wanted the chance to relearn who I was as I traveled and discovered the city, countryside, or wherever I would relocate. I had to step out of my comfort zone to see, that over the years, I lost myself.

Thirty-five

NEW YORK

I made my mind up! I was moving. I started to save money and look at places to live. I already knew where I was going...New York!!! From the time I visited when I was 15, I was in love with the city. I was traveling on tour with a community choir when I went there. I was enraptured by the culture, food, and whole experience. I was in heaven on earth. I had the opportunity to get back there. I used school as my ticket and excuse to move. I investigated different programs to enroll. I was interested in the fine arts, and surely New York was the appropriate place to learn. I forgot about my passion for nonprofits. It became a faint and distant memory as I thought of Broadway and the many stages and gigs I could get. My excitement about the opportunities to perform and have my name in lights on the marquee drowned the call to help and assist the less fortunate and the needs of the despondent.

I enrolled in CUNY, which is a community school in Manhattan. I enrolled in their Fine Arts degree program. Every step of the way was a challenge, more than I faced at other schools. I chalked it up to the fact that it was an out-of-town school. I had to fly to New York multiple times to fill out paperwork, take entry tests, and find housing. They wouldn't accept fax copies of anything. Either I had to mail it in or bring it in myself. I also had to call several offices to see if they had processed my applications or received transcripts. It seemed as if they were purposely losing my information or overlooking it. I was frustrated by the process. I had to check in daily to make sure they were moving along because I was on a timeline.

During that time, I called my mother. I wanted to get her thoughts about my move. I wasn't sure how she would take it, mainly since I hadn't asked or mentioned moving to her. I had no inkling on her temperament. Since I wasn't on speaking terms with God, I also wanted her to ask God to see if He approved the move to New York.

"Hello, mom."

"Hey baby, how are you?"

"I'm fine, and how are you doing?"

"I'm good, is everything okay?"

She sensed something was up.

"Everything is good. I just have a question and request for you."

"Okay..."

"I want to move to New York. I enrolled in school and plan on moving this January, but I wanted to speak to you first. I also wanted you to pray and see what God says to you please."

She paused as if she was taking it all in and processing the new information.

When she finally spoke, she simply said, "I will pray and let you know what God says."

She hung up the phone.

I continued to make plans to move. It was mid-November, and I had to hurry. I tried to make sure I did everything right. I made a checklist and consulted with others that moved to get their experiences. I wanted insight about what to be aware of as I organized my move.

I received my letter of acceptance into the program. I was elated. I acquired my school identification number and was able to log on as a student. It was becoming real to me. I nearly cried as I thought of my success. Then I remembered my mother didn't give me her blessing and call me back to tell me if God responded with an answer. I called her.

"Hello, mom! How are you?"

"Hey baby, I am good, and you?"

"I'm good. I was just wondering what happened to you calling me back about me moving to New York. Did you pray about it? Did God respond to your question, and if so, what did He say?"

"Yes baby, I did pray about it."

"Well then, why didn't you call me back mom?"

"Because I knew you wouldn't like the answer."

I felt unsettled by the pause, which seemed to last twenty minutes.

"I guess the Lord didn't approve?"

"No baby, He said, 'No,'"

"And did you tell Him how much I wanted to go?"

"I am sure He knows."

"And you didn't try to compel Him to let me go? You just gave up without a fight?"

"Look, if God said, 'No,' He means no. He has to have a good reason. I am sure it is not in His divine will. Maybe he's saving you from death."

I wasn't trying to hear that. I couldn't understand why she didn't intercede for what I wanted. I was her son for crying out loud. I wanted her to make God change His mind.

"This is why I didn't call you back. I knew you would be upset, and you are going to do what you want anyways, so I didn't see a need to be in a hurry to tell you what God said."

I was mystified and disappointed. I think I was more upset because I knew deep down, she was right. Whenever I set my mind to do something, I stop at nothing to do it. Against the odds, I wasn't to be defeated. It didn't matter what others said or if they agreed. I was going to have whatever it was I wanted. Despite what my mother told me, I continued to prepare for my move to New York. I created a timeline for the moving parts to ensure a foolproof move. I set my budget for the things I needed and made an inventory of the things to sell or give away. I started removing excess items in my apartment. I made a timeline to give notice to my landlord and place of employment. I looked up how to transfer my utilities and postal change address.

Everything was going as planned. I received a notification from the school that I could select my classes. Hurriedly, I logged on to pick the courses I wanted to take for the first semester. I then viewed my course schedule. I received an alert. They couldn't process my classes. I was advised to consult with the financial aid office. I knew I filled out my federal student aid forms. I was unclear about the issue. Perhaps it was yet another form needed to be signed or filled out. When I called the financial aid office to see what the problem was, they informed me I had loan that was in default status. I was stunned! I consolidated my debt to avoid any problems. As I pulled up my documentations regarding the consolidation, I asked her to verify the loan information. All of my loans were included in the consolidation except for one. It was overlooked. I was devastated. When I explained the situation to the financial aid office, they informed me they couldn't move forward until the issue was resolved. They gave me the numbers I needed to call to clear it up. It was another cog in my process, a big one. I banked my whole escape on getting into school. Without it, I felt helpless!

When I called the loan office, I was informed that indeed the loan was in default, and it wouldn't be removed from default status without going through a six-month process, which would be after my deadline to move and begin classes. I was horrified!! Everything I had done seemed for naught. I asked to speak to supervisors, but they sang the same song. I had to accept defeat. I was depressed. I was sure I was on my way to New York, but that dream was wrecked.

I spoke to my good friend Michael who lived in Atlanta, Georgia. I told him about how I felt deflated living in Milwaukee. I did everything I wanted to do and was ready to move. I was depressed and felt like my energy was depleted. He suggested that I consider moving to Atlanta and finishing school there. It wasn't what I wanted. Hotlanta didn't have a good reputation in Milwaukee's church world. The running joke was that men moved to Atlanta to *come out*. With several examples to prove their case, it was an unspoken truth. When a church-going Black man said they were relocating to Atlanta, their identity and fate were sealed. I couldn't have had it happen to me. I worked nearly thirty years to make sure my name was clean. I didn't want to be associated with the gay life. I was a preacher of the gospel who dedicated his life to ministry and church. I didn't want to throw it away by going to the Sodom and Gomorrah of the United States.

"I am not moving down there with you gays!"

"Why not?"

"Cause, I don't even like Atlanta!"

"Have you ever been?"

"Yes, when I was on tour with Wisconsin State Youth Choir. We were down there in the middle of Freaknik. It was horrible. We were on the tour bus to sing the gospel of Jesus Christ and Him crucified, and we ended up on the highway stuck in a traffic jam. And what did we see on the express way? We saw the heathens in the middle of the highway being ratchet with no underwear and halfway clothed. They were playing loud music and running on the highway from car-to-car drinking and smoking. It was Satan's den spewed upon the earth. Besides, you know whenever one of y'all moves there, everybody thinks y'all only moved there to be gay."

"What are you going to do then since you are against moving to Atlanta?"

"I don't know. I just got to get out of Milwaukee. I am over all of this. It's my job, church, life...just all of it! I am exasperated with these church folks and the games they play!"

"Okay, let me get this straight. Help me to understand because your ramblings don't make any sense! You say you are over these church people, but you won't move to Atlanta because of what they say. And you cannot go to New York. You had not one backup plan!" He wasn't done! "You didn't consider what you would do if New York fell through! And now, when I mentioned another option, you get hostile because of an experience that was one weekend of the year. You based the city off that, including the opinions of people you are tired of."

All I could do was sigh!

"You need to get your whiny ass together. There are plenty of schools and programs for you to enter. If you want to move down here, you know I will support you as well as Nathan! Oh yeah, how many people did you know in New York that could help you out? That's right, zero! Now, you get your ass online and look at options if you want to move and don't call me with more bullshit since I know you are much better and smarter than this!"

That conversation was just what I needed to refocus. I'm always grateful to have people around me that don't mind telling me the truth. I count them as a friend who will outright tell me what I need to hear versus what I want to hear. I won't grow or do better without honest feedback. He was right! I was allowing the thoughts of others to control my destiny.

When I got up from reliving my memory, I wondered if I made the right decision. Was it worth it? At the time, it felt like hell was purging the memories. Would Atlanta be better or just prove to be more of the same. I typed...

Thirty-six

DREAMLAND: GOD WINS AGAIN!

I had a dream. Three of my closest friends were at what appeared to be an obstacle course. At the beginning of the course, I noted the outfits we were wearing, and we looked comfortable. After going through a portion of the obstacle course, we met up again to discuss what we went through. They changed outfits. I didn't. After going through the next set, we reconnected. Two of my friends had on new outfits. It happened two more times.

"How is it that you all are changing outfits?"

They told me that not only were they changing outfits, but they came back to meet me because I was still in the same spot each time! When I awakened, I was thoroughly disturbed. What did my dream mean? What was happening? From my research and experience, I learned that many times in our dreams, we were warned or made aware of something we missed while awake. Whether it was a simple oversight or blatant disregard while awake, a dream was sent to make us cognizant. The morning of the dream, I went to work thinking about its meaning. I turned every detail over and over in my mind. I recalled the colors and my feelings. When I saw my friends change outfits, I was utterly frustrated because I was wearing the same thing, especially since I loved clothes so much. Further, why was I in the same spot? What did it mean?

I decided to go for a walk during my break. I still wasn't on speaking terms with God because He prevented me from going to New York. However, I knew I had to pay attention whenever I was sent a message. As I walked, I meditated on the dream. I was opening my mind and spirit and trying to reconnect with God to unearth what it meant. I used the portal of worship through music. In times past, music was a way to connect my spirit to God. My love for gospel music was embedded in me from as far back as I could remember. I remember waking up late at night at least four to five nights a week hearing either my mother praying or listening to music when I was a child. After a while, listening to gospel music and praying became routine. I was counting on it to work again. As I walked and began to spiritually align myself, I clearly heard an interpretation of the dream.

The dream referred to the journey of life. Simply put, while others around me were moving through life, I was stagnant. I thought I moved with others because I frequently saw them. In fact, they visited me where I remained. Whether mentally, spiritually, or physically stagnant or a combination, I became disillusioned enough to not recognize my own stillness. I kept on the same clothes, which indicated that I was unwilling to get stripped of my way of thinking or change and update my perspective. It was symbolic. I refused to get rid of baggage. The interpretation came to me as if I downloaded a file and was reading its transcription. As I read it, I felt uneasy. I wanted to refute and make excuses as to why I was motionless. If God would've let me move to New York, I wouldn't have been stagnant.

Just as I was compiling my list of reasons, a resounding rebuke echoed within, "I am desperately trying to get you to your destiny, and you are in my way!"

I shut up. The internal voice was commanding. I had no other option but to relinquish all rights to oppose the interpretation. Instead, I felt godly sorrow. It filled my heart and being. I knew what I had to do.

When I returned to my desk, I began to look at programs located in Atlanta, GA. I was determined to submit to the destiny designed for me. But there was a litmus test. If going to Atlanta was the course I was to take, I was going to see if it aligned with what my mother could affirm. I called her.

"Hello, mom."

"Hey baby, how are you?"

"I'm fine, and how have you been?"

"Yeah, I haven't heard from you in a while."

She had a motherly knowing and understood why I hadn't called since she told me God's response.

"Everything is good. I just have another question and request for you."

"Okay..."

"I want to move to Atlanta. I plan on enrolling in school and moving there this summer. I want you to pray and see what God says to you about this move."

This time she did not pause. Her response was immediate.

"God declared that you are released to go!"

"Huh? He said what?"

"Yeah, God said it is His will for you to go and He will make the way easy as you go."

"When did He say this to you?"

"As you were talking."

"Just like that?"

"Well, how long did you want Him to take. Obviously, you have things to get together, and I will be over to see what I want to take."

I was floored. It was okay for me to move to Atlanta but not to New York. I was excited and nervous. It became real! My transition to Atlanta was nothing like the way I had to plan for New York. I found a school with a program in leadership studies for nonprofits and applied. As custom to my nature, I called to verify and check the status of the documents I needed to send to the school. I was amazed. Every time I called an office, the person I spoke to had just finished the part of the process I was inquiring about. From processing my application, receiving my transcripts, to arranging room and board, everything was smooth, just as my mom said it would be.

Obtaining financial aid was my biggest worry and threat because of the obstacle that brought me down the last time. It had only been four months, and I didn't make any payments or attempt to reconcile the loan in default. When I called the financial aid office, I asked if they had processed my financial aid. They were just about to send it out in the mail. I viewed the documents online using my student identification. The amount of the financial aid award was sufficient to cover my expenses and more. I called the lending company to check on the defaulted loan to make sure nothing would be in my way. They were unable to find it. I asked several times just to make sure and provided the loan number. It was gone. My loans were consolidated, and I was eligible for financial aid.

"God Wins Again!"

I awakened and I knew I was on the right road. Going to Atlanta was the correct decision. I typed...

Thirty-seven

FIRST SUNDAY IN ATLANTA

Moving to Atlanta was a major move. I hadn't lived anywhere outside of Wisconsin. I had a relentless intention to finish school. I sold my car and vowed to concentrate on my education, which limited the places I could go. I decided to purchase a car when the time was right. I arrived on a Friday afternoon and spent the day taking tests and getting ready for classes. I got my books and listened to and watched the hustle and bustle of new students. I was settling in my new place, my new world. I was euphoric.

It was the first Sunday in Atlanta. I called my friend Nathan to bring me to church. My only stipulation was that it had to be a COGIC ministry. I was a third generation COGIC kid, and although I left the church I attended in Milwaukee, I thought starting anew in a different city would be optimal. Nathan obliged me and said he knew the *perfect* church to take me to. I found it interesting that he didn't go there. Nathan originally was Apostolic before he joined the COGIC church in Milwaukee and had no loyalty. His behavior was to be expected.

Going to church was a big deal. I found one of my best outfits and put it together ever so nicely. I was still not talking to God, but I refused to not attend church. I wanted to be in the presence of God but not interact with Him. Nathan picked me up on cue. He was excited that I moved to Atlanta. To tell you the truth, I was excited for the new venture and quest as well.

"I can't believe you are here!"

"Chile, I know. I can't believe it either! Now, what church are we going to? It's COGIC right?"

"Yes, and they are jumpin! I'm talkin bout straight church."

"Wait, what church do you go to?

"I go to Total Grace."

"Is that COGIC?"

"No, but they are just like a COGIC church. I think the pastor came from one. I know he was the music director for a well-known gospel singer before."

"Oh, okay. Then how did you find out about the church we are going to?"

"I've gone to many of their Sunday night services. A renowned prophet preached there several times, and every single time, the church was lit. We wouldn't leave until one or two in the morning. Even then, people would be in the parking lot still shouting and speaking in tongues. One time he said there was a lady named Kathy in the house. The church started looking around for Kathy. He then said, 'Kathy your husband has cancer.' A woman just started screaming. He said, 'Oh, that must be her.' Then he told her that he hadn't given her the prophecy yet. The church was already up. Then he told the woman because she started praising God without even hearing what He had to say, God was healing her husband right now. He told her that her husband was at home throwing up cancer right now. Then, he told her to come up there with the phone. When she got up there, he told her to call her husband. She did, and the husband answered. He told her to ask him if he was just throwing up. He responded that he was still in the bathroom from throwing up. Then the prophet asked her to ask her husband if the color was a milky green color. When she asked, the husband screamed, 'Yes.' The woman ran out of the church crying and screaming. The prophet told them to go check on her. He then took the phone and began to prophesy to the man on the phone. The church went bananas! It was over. We tore that church apart you hear me?"

"I bet y'all did! But that was an event. How do you know their Sunday morning service will be the same way?"

"Oh, I know. They have church like that all the time!"

"Okay Nathan."

As we were driving, I saw a nearby strip mall. For whatever reason, I hoped the church wasn't one of those storefront churches. And of course, it was. I couldn't believe we were pulling up to a little church. It wasn't that I was against small churches, as I grew up in small churches. I just thought from the stories Nathan told me that I was going to a larger church. The prophet wasn't a small name to bring into your church. Whenever the prophet came to Milwaukee, he was always at a big church, and it was packed out each time. Unless he didn't have as great a following here in Atlanta, I seriously doubted that small church could host him or the crowd he normally had. As well, it was my experience that in a smaller church, there was a higher risk of being singled out. Whether they had a word of prophecy or just wanted to acknowledge you, there was a tendency to be put on the spot. For those reasons, I felt a little deflated but just hoped for the best. As we pulled up there was only one other car there. I looked at my watch.

"What time do they start service?"

"They supposed to start at 10:45 a.m."

"Well, it's 11:00! Are you sure they didn't cancel service?"

"Naw! They are just late! You know how niggas do! Let's get something quick for breakfast and then we can come right back."

We went to a small restaurant and had breakfast for about 40 minutes. We were trying to give them a chance to show up and get started. When we returned, they already began service. We walked in while praise and worship was going on. A man was singing congregational songs without backup singers. It was reminiscent of my childhood how on Friday nights and before we had a praise team on Sundays, one of the church mothers or missionaries broke out with a congregational.

We sat in our seats along with 25 others in that little box church. I felt compelled to participate for fear they would think I was a non-convert. I stood and sang along and did my part to appear interested in the service. After about 10 minutes of calling on Jesus tarrying style, I noticed God's presence hadn't shown up. As I looked around, there was one older lady who appeared to be feeling the spirit. I wondered what she was feeling because it was dry as bleached bones. I later learned she was related to the man leading worship. After another 10 minutes of incessant Jesus calling, I became a bit annoyed. Why are we still here in this same song? Is he stalling for the pastor? Is he waiting for more people to show up? Mostly, why is Jesus not here? I was used to storefront churches having knock-down, drag-out services, especially when they called out Jesus' name in succession. I couldn't shake that I felt nothing. It reminded me of the Bible story of Elijah on Mount Carmel with the 450 prophets of Baal. As the showdown between Elijah and the prophets of Baal went forward, the prophets of Baal called on Baal for hours on end, but nothing happened. After many hours, Elijah mocked the prophets and said, "Cry aloud...either he is talking, or he is pursuing, or he is in a journey, or peradventure he sleepeth, and must be awakened," (1 Kings 18:27). The Baal prophets whipped themselves into a frenzy, lacerating themselves with swords and spears, anything to get Baal to respond. But nothing came. That is how I felt at that COGIC church.

Finally, I turned to Nathan.

"Who is this man and why won't the pastor come out and end this madness?"

"That is the pastor?"

"I know you lying!"

"No, I'm serious!"

"Get me out of here! If Jesus refuses to show up for the pastor after he has called Him for 25 minutes, then I refuse to let him speak a word over my life during the message. I don't know if Jesus is boycotting this place, but I am not staying here!"

"Okay, we can leave after offering."

As we marched around for offering, we marched right out the door.

As we were going to the car, I asked Nathan, "What the hell was that?"

"Honestly, I don't know. That was the first time its happened. First of all, there was no one there. Secondly, I don't know where the praise and worship leader was. I hate the way the pastor sounds. He thinks he can sing, and he sounds hideous."

"I wasn't as concerned about how he sounded. We chanted Jesus for 89 minutes and no Jesus was there. Really? He is the pastor, and God is not responding to him. He cannot do surgery on my soul! Take me anywhere where Jesus is! I shouldn't have asked for a specific COGIC church."

Okay! I know just where to take you."

When we pulled up to the next church, I saw cars parked everywhere. The church was in a large cathedral-style building. I immediately began to smile and thought that at least my outfit wouldn't go to waste. As we walked up to the church, I heard the blaring sounds of the music thickening the atmosphere, which reminded me of churches in Chicago. The quality of sound was recognizable and compelling. I could feel myself being drawn in and I quickened my pace to the church. It was packed! The balcony was full. From the hallway, I peered into the pulpit and saw a man singing congregational call-and-response songs. I thought it was the old-school congregational song day in Atlanta. It felt like the man picked up where the last church left off. However, there was one stark difference. The energy and presence of God was evident.

The usher found us seats on the third row from the front. As we set out to our seats, I tried to take in the scenery. People were worshipping, rocking side to side to the cadence of the music. Their hands were waving in the air in sheer exaltation as they shouted, "Hallelujah, glory to God, yes Lord, and thank you." The charge in the atmosphere was unmistakably the work of God. I couldn't help but feel absolutely at home as the sound of the saints was reverberating. It seemed to be what I was looking for. It wasn't COGIC, but it met the criteria of God being there, which is much more important.

We sat behind a Caucasian young man who looked like he was maybe 17 through 19 years old. He was right along with the rest of the congregants. He responded to the shifts of the spirit and had the noted looks and moves of the Black Pentecostal church. It was unbelievable to me just how well he emulated what I grew up with in the Black culture. From the jerking of his body, which was referred to as quickening, to the waving trembling hands around in a circle fashion. He had us down to a science.

I tried to look around my surroundings as we sang. I couldn't help but notice a theme. I was trying not to be an obvious visitor. I use a strategy in my perusal of the attendees. Amidst the praise, worship, and shouting, was a differentness. Now, I knew they said that Atlanta was the Black gay mecca. I was also aware that homosexuals were usually attracted to high-spirited services and good music. It stood with a good reason why the aesthetic of the church looked as it did. The stereotypical look of the gay community was abounding in that church. The more I looked around, the more I saw men wearing summer scarves and broaches and carrying man-bags. Some men had on make-up, bangles, and other feminine accessories.

Some of the women looked suspicious too. A female usher walked by wearing a man's suit. I looked down in inspection of the lady. She had on men's' expensive zoot suit like shoes. I wondered why they let her serve like that. She clearly didn't have the right spirit! But she was not alone. That church carried the spirit of homosexuality.

I began to ponder on my great concern. Perhaps that was why the Spirit of the Lord was strong in the midst. He was there to clean up the mess, and a mess it was. Everywhere I looked were groups and clusters of those people. God had work ahead of Him. I felt bad for the pastor but knew if God allowed me to come to this church, it was for a reason, and I knew God wouldn't put more on a person than what they could handle. The man who led the worship and praise ended his portion and went to his seat. From where his seat was positioned, I supposed he was the pastor. I turned to Nathan and confirmed my suspicion. I thought it was odd that the pastor of such a large congregation would lead praise and worship. But hey, who was I to judge?

The announcing clerk took the stage.

"This is the day that the Lord has made, let us rejoice. I said let us rejoice! Giving honor to God who is the head of my life. We are certainly glad to be in the midst of a great service today. We also honor our pastor.

The people stood to their feet, clapped, and cheered.

"And we also honor the first gentleman!"

Again, the people clapped and cheered.

Wait! What is a first gentleman? I hadn't heard the term. It was my first Sunday in Atlanta. I wasn't aware of the different naming conventions. I've been in church all my life and have heard various names for preachers, but I hadn't heard of a first gentleman. I was alerted, it just felt weird for some reason.

"Did they call him the first gentleman?"

Nathan was laughing after I asked the question. I was only interested in the answer. I put on hold the thought that Nathan had something to do with the confusion in my mind.

"Yes, they did."

"Is that the assistant pastor?"

"No, it ain't?"

"Then who is that man?"

I asked almost as if I knew the answer but refused to allow the thoughts to enter my world without assistance. Through a veil of tears running down Nathan's face and laughter inappropriate for church, he told the answer.

"That is his husband!"

I believe I suspended myself in mid-air in my mind. Impossible! I had a mixture of utter disbelief, horror, and devastation.

"What do you mean?"

"That man is married to the pastor you just said was anointed!"

I thought an aneurism would happen to me right there. I recently read about another celebrated pastor attending an affirming church conference in Florida. It was all over the saint's lips how far he had left the faith. He started telling people that were living a life unpleasing to the Lord they were going to heaven and fine just the way they were. How could this be happening to me? Why would Nathan trick me like that? He knew I was totally against it. I wasn't about to play with God. I honored and believed the Word of God. He condemned homosexuality and I followed his principles.

Nathan and I had been friends for at least 15 years. He saw me transition from high school, through my first college experience, and though St. Emmanuel. He knew how seriously I took God. He hadn't allowed me in his vehicles, claiming for some reason, that God listened to me, and I always spoke against him when he was about to sin or do something wrong. I was known in the gospel music community as a person who, as others described me, sent people to their spiritual corner. As well, they hated for me to be around whenever they were planning to do something I deemed sinful. I spoke against it, and oddly strange things happened and prevented them from doing whatever it was they had desired to do. Nathan was among those who claimed I was a no-nonsense preacher.

For the life of me, I couldn't get why Nathan thought it was okay to bring me to that church, the modern-day Sodom and Gomorrah. I only knew of churches where gay people seemed to like and enjoy going. I hadn't been to a church where they taught gay was okay. It was hypocrisy at its finest. I immediately started talking to the Father!

"Lord, you know good-and-well I had no idea about this church. I may not be in a good place with you right now, but I would *never* come to church to play with you. I reverence your name and wouldn't make a mockery out of your house. I'm not sure why you even allowed it to happen or what I'm supposed to learn from this. This is crazy! And it would be just my luck today you would send your angels down to torch this place as you did with Sodom and Gomorrah."

I mean, my life's work in the church could die such an abominable death, with no fault of my own. But who's going to believe it? As messy as the church folk and saints were, they would just be waiting to hear I was in the number that was destroyed by God's wrath and anger. I could hear it now: "I always knew he was gay! I was never fooled. That's why he moved down to Atlanta; you know it's the black gay capital!" It was too much! Who could give my side of the story? Who could plead my cause? The only witness who could help would be dead with me. Those thoughts were racing in my head until an interruption happened. The pastor had the mic again and picked up where he left off. I missed the rest of the announcements, offering, and choir selection.

This time the pastor sang a worship ballad, and the church followed along. True to the promise of people with one accord, the Holy Spirit manifested once again. I could no longer participate in the sacrilegious behavior. I couldn't move but looked at each member. I was trying to understand what possessed them to be so reprobate. I thought it was just like the narrative in the Bible in Genesis 18 when God sent an angel to warn that He was going to destroy the land because of their wickedness.

Abraham approached and said, "Will You indeed sweep away the righteous with the wicked? Suppose there are fifty righteous people within the city; will You indeed sweep *it* away and not spare the place for the sake of the fifty righteous who are in it? Far be it from You to do such a thing, to kill the righteous with the wicked, so that the righteous and the wicked are *treated* alike. Far be it from You! Shall not the Judge of all the earth deal justly?" So the LORD said, "If I find in Sodom fifty righteous within the city, then I will spare the entire place on their account." And Abraham replied, "Now behold, I have ventured to speak to the Lord, although I am *only* dust and ashes. Suppose the fifty righteous are lacking five, will You destroy the entire city because of five?" And He said, "I will not destroy *it* if I find forty-five there." And he spoke to Him yet again and said, "Suppose forty are found there?" And He said, "I will not do *it* on account of the forty." Then he said, "Oh may the Lord not be angry, and I shall speak; suppose thirty are found there?" And He said, "I will not do *it* if I find thirty there." And he said, "Now behold, I have ventured to speak to the Lord; suppose twenty are found there?" And He said, "I will not destroy *it* on account of the twenty." Then he said, "Oh may the Lord not be angry, and I shall speak only this once: suppose ten are found there?" And He said, "I will not destroy *it* on account of the ten." (Genesis 18:23-32, NASB)

Since I could sense the powerful presence of the Lord in the place, I knew He had to be there because of some righteous persons. I looked around and saw the mothers. Perhaps there were enough of them pleading for grace and mercy that God held back His hand of judgment. But there were only five mothers. I wondered who the other remnants of believers God was honoring.

After the second movement of the Spirit, the pastor began his message. My head hurt from trying to reason what was going on. I couldn't help but be conflicted as to why the presence of God would be there. I was always taught that God wouldn't dwell in an unclean temple. The pastor was living in sin with another man. I knew about plenty of pastors in the same type of relationship. They just didn't broadcast it or publicly acknowledge it. But this pastor was bold to lead a congregation in open sin! The aggregation of members also celebrated his behavior. They stood and honored this transgression. I wondered what type of witchery it was. Why did I feel such a powerful move of God? The anointing was to flow from the head down according to the Old Testament. It flowed from the crown of the pastor's head into his beard and poured downward. How was it possible for him to be in an openly homosexual relationship and be used to allow the oil of God to flow during his worship segment?

The pastor transitioned to give the message. I was gravely concerned. I didn't believe he was going to have anything more than a bunch of church jargon and fluff. Perhaps it was a mistake that the anointing fell twice in one service by that wolf in sheep's clothing. But wait! He wasn't hiding anything. Unsure as to what to make of it, I decided to endure his message. As the pastor spoke, I was amazed at his words. Not only were they filled with revealing information relevant to the needs of my life, but I knew beyond a shadow of a doubt, he had been in the face of God. Of course, being a preacher myself, having heard some of the best preachers and some of the worst, I knew the differences between pure performance and actual anointing. Many preachers are gifted inspirational speakers. They know how to lace together words to move and inspire their audiences. Others were witty in the calisthenics of the Pentecostal Black church. They knew how to whoop and drive a point to tickle the emotions of the people. Some had the gift and anointing. Those who didn't, relied on their laurels to get through the message. But to have their ears to the mouth of God to hear what He would say...that was exactly what was undeniable about his message.

I was devastated. How could it be? It went against everything I knew. My theology stood strong against it. God and I weren't on speaking terms, so I refused to directly ask Him to clarify what was going on. Plus, I had dedicated my whole life to God and church. I should have had some kind of reference for it, but I didn't. On some level I felt insulted yet was intrigued. It was too much for my first Sunday in Atlanta. After church, we stopped to get something to eat. I went home, ate my meal, took two pain pills, and went directly to bed. When I awakened, I still was in disbelief. I wasn't ready to ask God about it. I typed...

Thirty-eight

RAPED BY GOD

The summer of 2009 was one for the books. I signed up for four classes at school. Each instructor challenged me. They seemed to spiritually have it out for me. I understood it was a Christian School, but I was there for the non-profit and parachurch leadership program, not for a spiritual awakening. Little did I realize, there was a great conspiracy to move me into my destiny. One night, as I was preparing for bed, I listened to gospel music, which helped to settle and lull me to sleep. As I was drifting off, "Every Knee Shall Bow" by the L.A. Mass Choir was played over the radio. I shot my hands in the air and tears started pouring down my face like torrents of rain. When I opened my mouth, all tongues gushed out. The Spirit overtook my whole room. It was unlike any tarrying service I had experienced. I was still not talking to God. I was mad but overcome by the power of God. I felt it externally and internally. I didn't have time to resist. I rolled on my floor, wept, and spoke in tongues for about an hour. I wasn't sure if my roommates heard me or not. They didn't disturb me.

It was a battle between me and God. He entered without warning or permission, as if I were raped. Now, some would say you cannot rape the willing. I would say I'm sure I was playing hard to get at that time. I was engulfed in His awesomeness. I could hardly breathe and had to admit I surely missed that type of encounter. When it subsided, I crawled back to my bed. As soon as I closed my eyes, I saw VISION in rainbow colors stretched across the sky. I immediately knew what it was about. It had been months since I went to the church with the pastor who had a husband, and the presence of God was there! I wasn't in a place to talk to God about it then and get an understanding, seeing as I wasn't on good terms with God. I was much too hurt from my Milwaukee experience to rekindle a relationship. After months of recuperating, I was ready! I sat up in the bed and talked with God.

"Yes...about that church...why where you there?"

The Holy Spirit was silent.

"I mean, we were taught that you don't dwell in an unclean temple and start with the head and go downward, even as the anointing fell from the pastor's head onto his beard then saturated the rest of his garments. You are a God of order. That church had a pastor who was openly defiant against the Word! I don't understand why were you there? I mean, homosexuality is a sin! The abominable sin to some, but sin nonetheless!"

I could feel myself getting worked up and decided to take a breath.

God answered with a calm still voice, "Is it as sin?"

I couldn't believe the question. Is it a sin? Was God being funny or facetious? I got out of my bed and sat on the floor. My head was spinning. I had a myriad of answers to the question posed. Yet, I was more concerned with the rationale for asking the question.

"What do you mean is it? Your word says it is a sin!"

"Show me."

What's happening here? What' going on? I couldn't fathom the purpose of the request. Where's this going? I knew from past experiences that God always had a reason. I had to take the road to see where it ended up. I just hoped I wouldn't be devastated by what I found. I opened my Bible to the most notorious story apropos for the situation: Sodom and Gomorrah. I turned to Genesis 19. I read the whole chapter to find the verse where homosexuality was condemned and how God destroyed the two cities because of it. I read and reread the chapter. Hmm, I couldn't find it. I had been a student of the Bible all my life, and I knew it was here. I heard the story way too many times for it not to be. I must have read it in haste and missed it. I read it yet again...nothing. I decided to read the pericope of the text. I read the chapter before and the chapter after and found nothing. "I don't believe this...it's not here," I thought. But where did they get it from? They may not have been the savviest, but I don't think the whole church across Christendom made it up! I reread the text, looking for what could be confused as God being against homosexuality. I found it! Verse four.

"But before they lay down, the men of the city, even the men of Sodom, compassed the house round, both old and young, all the people from every quarter" (Genesis 19:4, KJV). That's where they said the men were on the porch looking for the men that went into Lot's house. However, the text, when looked at grammatically, had no credence to the resolution. The Biblical scribers followed grammatical structure and rules. The gender pronouns were male. Because the last reference to those who were on the porch says people, which is an inclusive reference, the distinction nullifies the theory of it being only men on the porch.

I wanted to further investigate using additional resources I learned about when I was a student at the Bible College. I referenced the original Hebrew words from the text and sure enough, each time the English word man was used, it was originally mankind in Hebrew. That was just one big ole orgy. I couldn't believe it! I was mortified. All these years I was fed a lie. I became more inquisitive and wasn't done with God. Homosexuality is still a sin, for it says so in Leviticus and Deuteronomy. I found passages where homosexuality, wearing blended fabrics, eating pigs, and all sorts of other things were condemned. Yet, in today's time, it's practiced. I became overwhelmed. What have we been doing? Why was this okay? I then thought, "Wait! It's still in the New Testament. Off to the New Testament I went. I looked up what effeminate spirit meant. I did my research and found it referred to the watering down of the gospel, not homosexuality. I was dumbfounded.

I read verse by verse, looking up and researching the Scriptures used to demonize me and others. I couldn't believe I had been hoodwinked, bamboozled, and taken. I slid out of my chair while holding the Bible in my lap and cried. I sobbed for more than an hour. The funny thing is that I didn't cry for myself. Although my life was undeniably challenged because of the stigma attributed to homosexuality, I cried for the people I knew the church condemned and they died by their own hands. As their last hope, they went to the church and was shunned and demonized. They were told it was their fault. I wept for hours. What did that mean? I started journaling the Scriptures and my findings. I typed...

Thirty-nine

APOLOGY TO THE CHURCH

Through my journey during the summer of 2009, I had time to reflect. Without any preexisting distractions from the demands of life, I was able to clear my mind. My mental purging began. My ideologies and theologies were challenged and/or confirmed. I heard the same message embedded within the lessons in each class I attended. Everywhere I turned, I learned a lesson and received a message. Somehow, the professor rang on about forgiveness in each lecture. Not only that, as I attended church on Sunday, the same theme was preached.

God, like always, used all areas of my life to point me to the message he needed me to receive. Little by little I started to concede. One time, while listening to gospel music, I prayed a short prayer, but a prayer, nonetheless. As I continued listening to gospel music and meditating, I heard an impression on my heart transmitted through the Spirit.

"Write a personal apology letter to every member of St. Emmanuel!"

The message was so matter of fact that I could not deny its existence. That was absurd. It had to have been blatantly sent in error! How could it be possible that I needed to write a letter of apology? If anything, the church owed me an apology!

"I know you lying! Why the hell would I write an apology letter?"

All the *hell* they put me through! All the years I dedicated and sacrificed to that church! All the hours and thousands of dollars I spent to make sure I did more than my part to keep the church going!

"I know you kidding!"

That isn't even funny. I spent my entire twenties working, cooking, cleaning, praying, participating in shut-ins, fasting, decorating, casting out devils, healing, attending, and running revivals. And for what? In the end, I came out bitter, broken, dishearten, disenchanted, and disinterested.

"Now you want me to write a letter to apologize?"

"So, you did everything right? You never were trouble? You never intentionally tried to tear up the church? Never did you start arguments, antagonized members, or advised with selfish motives? Never were you dishonorable in your actions? Never did you try to take away others' self-esteem for your ego's sake? Was it not you on assignment to take down the pastor before you were converted and knocked off your beast? I'm sure you remember when you sought to sabotage the church. Your motives weren't pure, and you did all you could to terrorize that church. You write the letter to free your own soul."

I knew the Spirit was correct. Sometimes guilt hides in pointing fingers. It was much easier to blame and point fingers at others than to deal with my personal indiscretions. I was humbled by the conviction of the Holy Spirit. I recalled how merciless I was upon entering the church. My heart was cold and callous. I allowed my pain and bitterness from the mistreatment by leaders of the church to harden my heart. I argued points in Bible study or Sunday school just for the sake of trying to prove the teacher didn't know as much as they thought they did. I wanted to unarm anyone with authority by insulting their knowledge to teach. Since I had been a student of the word from a young child, it was a joy to do. I always challenged what my Sunday school teacher taught. However, back then, it was innocent. I just wanted an understanding and sometimes what they taught just simply did not add up.

Although I grew up with most of the members of the church, there was just no satisfying my thirst to uproot everyone and play like it was their fault. I used the church as a ploy to employ the church members to have to put up with me. Their love of God compelled them to not excommunicate me. My social miscreant ways muddled with egotistical attitude was a never-failing thorn during my beginning phase of the church. My assignment was to write a personal letter to the old members of the church. We were a small church, and I knew the letters were to go to the core members of about 25. However, I didn't have the means to mail them. I told the Spirit I would write the letters knowing I couldn't afford to mail them. I was only working a temporary job and had little money to spare. I wrote the letters one by one.

The next day I went to work as normal. When my boss came in, she looked at me.

"Do you use stamps?"

"Not really, but I can always use them."

I knew one or a couple of stamps wouldn't cover the cost to mail all the letters.

"No, it's an interesting story. I always order a book of stamps because I do a lot of mailing. I paid for the book but when I got in the car there was a book and two rolls of stamps. You can have a roll if you want, it's like 100 stamps."

All I could do is smile in defeat. I had no choice but to concede. God, who is the author and provider of all, had won again. I immediately sent the letters.

In about a week, I received a call from my best friend in Milwaukee.

"Nigga, what are these letters you are sending out and where's mine at?"

"What are you talking about?"

I forgot the letters or any reason why he would have known about them.

"Naw nigga, don't be actin' like you don't know what I'm talking about?"

"I don't know about what you speak of?"

"I was riding in the car on the way to Chicago for our New G rehearsal and Shay turned to Anthony and asked if he had gotten a letter from you this week. He turned to Shay and said, 'Yeah.' They were trying to figure out why you sent it. They thought maybe you were sick and were dying. I asked what they were talking about. They said you had sent them all these letters apologizing for all the things you did to them at St. Emmanuel. Is that correct?"

"That is correct but why didn't they call or ask me about the letters if they had questions? After all, I sent the letter."

"Well, bae I don't know! But what I want to know is where is my letter? Did you need my address?"

"Why would I send you a letter? You were never a part of St. Emmanuel. In fact, you were against me being a member."

"Now wait one minute! Why would you say I was against you being a member?"

"Because every time you dropped me off at the church, you berated me and asked why I was at the little storefront with all the power I had."

"Well, that's beside the point, I want to know where my letter is. Get a pen and paper and write my address down. I need my letter with full apologies for the trauma and nastiness I had to endure."

"Sir, stop this! I was never nasty to you, nor did you have to endure any trauma."

"Yes, you did! You taunted me by calling me twisted and told me I was going to hell!"

"You were twisted and are still on your way to hell! You will not be getting a letter and that's final. The Lord did not ask for it, and if you want one, type it yourself but be sure to sign your name."

"Fine! But your little letter ain't gonna save you from your little strange fire church!"

"Either way, no letter for you!"

I was feeling dejected. No one I sent the letter responded, not even to indicate they received the letter.

"You did send the letters to clear you, correct?"

I adjusted my expectation and then my attitude. Soon after, I received a message from the person I least expected to hear from.

"Hey David, just wanted to let you know I received your letter. I want to say, "Thank you!" I stopped going to church because of all the hypocrisy I saw first-hand in the church. To be honest, you were one of the few persons I thought was genuine and loved the Lord. Because of this letter, I am going to go back to church and just love God for myself."

As I read the response, I began to cry. It was worth it for just one person to have been touched and changed. That was unlike the other memories. First, it was the same summer it happened. I sat up wondering. Why this memory? I was grateful for the chance to experience the path of forgiving and letting go but was equally coming to understand the power and humility of asking forgiveness in a unique situation. I went to the computer and typed...

Forty

BORN OUT OF PAIN

Yes, I was born out of pain...

Pain of rejection

Pain of degradation

Pain of self-sabotage

Pain of feeling less than

Pain of worthlessness

Pain of failure

Pain of fear

Pain of loneliness

Pain of panic

Pain of mistrust

Pain of distress

Pain of shame

Pain of rage

Yes, it hurt like hell! Yes, some days the memories feel just as strong as the actual events. I reflected on the various events that have helped to shape and make me into the person I am today. I lament many experiences, but I am grateful. It was necessary. It was good for me that I was afflicted because I was able to find the strength.

I am still dealing with the emotional and psychological ramifications of my myriad of traumas. I have discovered the root of my behaviors and am making modifications to be the best me I can be. I am ever grateful for the collage of my life that both tore me apart and restored me.

I may have been born out of pain, but I was also born into destiny!

- Selah!

ABOUT THE AUTHOR

David Glover is an organizational psychologist and founder of Ennoblement, LLC, a consulting company. He and created the initiative I Like Me, which is a social-emotional learning development program.

David has taught hundreds of executives and other professionals and has given keynote speeches to more than 200 groups. He is a certified Executive and Life Coach and an American Association of Christian Counselors (AACC) member in good standing and a member of the Society of Industrial and Organizational Psychologists (SIOP).

He is the author of an award-winning book entitled *Building and Maintaining Organizations*. David travels as a public speaker and spreads hope. With a message of self-acceptance, self-awareness, and anti-bullying, he aims to raise mental health awareness. As a consultant, he offers his expertise to strengthen organizations with pragmatic approaches to yield the best cultures and comradery. Whether he is functioning as a public speaker, consultant, elocutionist, David is vested in the belief, that you can change individual lives, cultures, and the world!

David completed his bachelor's degree from Beulah Heights University in Atlanta, Georgia in leadership studies with a dual concentration in biblical studies and psychology. He earned his master's degree in industrial-organizational psychology, with a concentration on executive coaching. He is a proud graduate of Touro University where he earned his doctorate in human and organizational psychology.

Contact

bornoutofpain22@gmail.com

www.drdavidnglover.net